Inheriting Walter Benjamin

Walter Benjamin Studies

In this series devoted to the writings of Walter Benjamin each volume will focus on a theme central to contemporary work on Benjamin. The series aims to set new standards of work on Benjamin available in English for students and researchers in Philosophy, Cultural Studies and Literary Studies.

Series Editor: Andrew Benjamin, Professor of Philosophy and Jewish Thought, Monash University, Australia and Anniversary Chair in the Department of the Humanities at Kingston University, UK.

Inheriting Walter Benjamin

Gerhard Richter

Bloomsbury Academic
An imprint of Bloomsbury Publishing Plc

B L O O M S B U R Y
LONDON · OXFORD · NEW YORK · NEW DELHI · SYDNEY

Bloomsbury Academic

An imprint of Bloomsbury Publishing Plc

50 Bedford Square   1385 Broadway
London   New York
WC1B 3DP   NY 10018
UK   USA

www.bloomsbury.com

BLOOMSBURY and the Diana logo are trademarks of Bloomsbury Publishing Plc

First published 2016
© Gerhard Richter, 2016

Gerhard Richter has asserted his right under the Copyright, Designs and Patents Act, 1988, to be identified as Author of this work.

A version of Chapter 3 was originally published as a journal article, 'Benjamin's Blotting Paper: Writing and Erasing a Theological Figure of Thought', *Symposium* 65:1 (2011); an earlier version of Chapter 4 appeared in *Sparks Will Fly: Benjamin and Heidegger*, ed. Andrew Benjamin and Dimitris Vardoulakis (Albany: SUNY Press, 2015); a version of Chapter 5 was published in *Grey Room* (MIT Press) 39 (Spring 2010); Chapter 6 was originally published in German in *Benjamins Grenzgänge—Benjamin's Frontiers*, ed. Gerhard Richter, Karl Solibakke, and Bernd Witte (Würzburg: Königshausen & Neumann, 2013).

British Library Cataloguing-in-Publication Data

A catalogue record for this book is available from the British Library.

ISBN: HB: 9781474251242
PB: 9781474251235
ePDF: 9781474251259
ePub: 9781474251266

Library of Congress Cataloging-in-Publication Data

A catalog record for this book is available from the Library of Congress.

Series: Walter Benjamin Studies

Typeset by Fakenham Prepress Solutions, Fakenham, Norfolk NR21 8NN
Printed and bound in India

Contents

1

Inheriting Benjamin Otherwise

Are we still inheriting Walter Benjamin? Will we ever stop inheriting him? What would it mean to stop inheriting Benjamin? What would it mean to have inherited him in the first place? If I were permitted a confessional moment, I would say that inheriting Benjamin, for me, is always also a self-inheritance. I was first introduced to Benjamin by an enlightened philosophy teacher in *Gymnasium*. This teacher had a special interest in the Frankfurt School and the history of philosophy with which it engages, and he read Plato, Descartes, Hegel, and others with us. One day in eleventh grade – when we had just finished reading *To Have or To Be?* by Erich Fromm and *Dialectic of Enlightenment* by Horkheimer and Adorno – the philosophy teacher unpacked a stack of yellow-greenish Suhrkamp paperbacks, announcing that we would be reading 'The Work of Art in the Age of Its Technical Reproducibility' by someone named Benjamin for the next few weeks. Baffled by the writer's apodictic and refractory way of thinking and writing, yet already sensing a deep affinity for his penetrating and poetic tropes, I began – slowly, laboriously and always, I felt, altogether incompletely – to inherit Benjamin.

What the essays gathered in the present volume add to my ongoing attempts at inheriting Benjamin over the past three decades is the double perspective whereby each reading attends to an issue raised in Benjamin's writing while at the same time reflecting on the challenges that these issues present for the process of inheritability and transmissibility. In other words, with each turn to a specific Benjaminian passage, the chapters in this book not only engage their respective tropes, they also inquire into the conditions of possibility that reading and inheriting his corpus pose for us today. Each chapter reads Benjamin and watches itself reading Benjamin, participating in the act of inheriting his resistant legacy while seeking to pose the question of inheritance in relation to the Benjaminian archive always one more time.

No act of inheriting Benjamin could situate an heir in the position of mere successor. At least not if by successor what is meant is someone who receives a self-identical legacy consisting of fully transparent and comprehensible precepts that could be implemented at will – say, a systematically unified account of language, a set of stable political concepts or a remainderless philosophy of history. It is no accident that already the young Hegel observes, 'with regard to the inner essence of philosophy, there are neither predecessors nor successors [*in Rücksicht aufs innere Wesen der Philosophie gibt es weder Vorgänger noch Nachgänger*].'[1] This is so, in part, because philosophy is the site, according to Hegel's logic, in which reason reflects on itself, an activity in which a core set of concerns is self-reflexively engaged over and over, regardless of the individual thinker who acts as the agent or site of reflection in any particular instance. Yet Hegel's sentiment also problematizes the very notion of intellectual heritage, rather than assuming that it is self-evident and requires no further consideration.

Hegel's apodictic statement should resonate with readers of Benjamin in our time. After all, there is nothing at all self-evident about the notion that we should know how to inherit the thinking and writing of Benjamin today. To be sure, the fascination with his style of thinking and writing continues, inviting ever-renewed acts of readerly inheritance. In fact, Benjamin's thinking itself is rooted in the conviction that an inheritance is not only mediated *by* language but takes place *in* language. As he writes in a fragment on the mode of inheritance we call translation: 'There is no world of thought that is not a world of language, and one only sees of the world what is presupposed by language [*Es gibt keine Gedankenwelt, die nicht eine Sprachwelt wäre, und man sieht nur das an Welt, was durch die Sprache vorausgesetzt ist*].'[2] This preconditioning by language requires constant attunement to the textual basis of cognition, a perpetual interpretation and reinterpretation of the ways in which language makes the world what it appears to us.

It is this abiding engagement with language – both Benjamin's, and ours with Benjamin's language – that structures the experience of inheriting his words. As Howard Eiland and Michael W. Jennings put it in their recent critical biography of Benjamin, when considering the question as to why his 'works still speak so compellingly to the general reader and the scholar alike' today:

> It was Benjamin's genius to find the forms within which a profundity and complexity fully comparable to that of contemporaries such as Heidegger and Wittgenstein could resonate through an immediately engaging and memorable prose. Reading him is therefore a sensory, no less than intellectual, experience. It is like the first taste of a tea-soaked madeleine: dimly remembered worlds blossom in the imagination. And as the phrases linger, constellate, and begin permutation, they subtly attune themselves to an emerging recombinatory logic, slowly releasing their destabilizing potential.[3]

Surely, the singular intellectual and sensory pleasures that the Benjaminian archive continues to provide along with its destabilizing insights will provoke a continued engagement with his ghostly legacy. Even when Benjamin composes pedagogical radio talks for children or when he merely scribbles, as during his 1934 drug experiments with the addiction researcher Fritz Fränkel, the fascination of his writing continues to captivate readers.[4]

Yet there are also cases of Benjamin's (now former) readers turning their back on him, after finding themselves unwilling or unable to continue this inheriting. For instance, the well-known German critical theorist and media scholar Norbert Bolz, who not only wrote his dissertation on the aesthetic theory of Benjamin's friend Adorno but also has published a series of influential essays and books on Benjamin himself, recently confessed: 'I have my doubts. I am no longer able to learn anything from Adorno or Benjamin.'[5] To be sure, an heir can always refuse to inherit, though the nature of a particular inheritance may not leave one any choice in the matter, imposing itself, even inflicting itself, on the one who is to receive it. It is as though the strange inheritance that Benjamin's often apodictic, melancholy and refractory thoughts and sentences bequeath upon us are not easy to accommodate into our received intellectual registers, especially today, some three-quarters of a century after his premature death following Nazi persecution.

At times it would seem easier to disown the inheritance of this enigmatic thinker by making *him* disinherit *us*, by rejecting a legacy or tradition of thinking that self-consciously refuses to yield the stable insight of a self-identical system of concepts. Perhaps the question for us as heirs of Benjamin is how we can inherit him today by looking at our own predicaments from *his* vantage point instead of reducing him to a category, this or that perceived instrumentality, function or 'usefulness' with respect to other motives. Such a shift in perspective would have nothing to do with uncritical piety or even hagiography. Slavoj Žižek puts it well when he avers that 'when we are dealing with a truly great philosopher, the real question to be raised concerns not what this philosopher may still tell us, what he may still mean to us, but rather the opposite, namely, what *we* are, what our contemporary situation might be, in *his* eyes, how our epoch would appear to *his* thought.'[6] Turning the telescope the other way, as it were, opens up possibilities for inheriting that have remained unthought.

Inheriting an intellectual legacy, particularly in Benjamin's work, is not a self-evident given – a transaction to be initiated and completed whenever we choose – but rather an open question. As he writes in the early sketch '*Trauerspiel* and Tragedy': 'The time of history is infinite in every direction and unfulfilled at every moment. This means that no single empirical event is thinkable that would stand in a necessary relationship to the particular historical situation in which it was produced.'[7] Far from assuming an a-historicist perspective vis-à-vis an event, Benjamin wishes to emphasize the ways in which a possible *relationship* to an event becomes a matter of inheriting it, that is, learning to read it and to relate to it in a way that is unforeseeable and that requires acts of interpretation for which the inheriting subject could not have been prepared in advance. In other words, our understanding of the relationship between a textual utterance or other phenomenon and its particular historical situation is not foreclosed a priori by an alleged necessity, but rather is a matter of learning how to read and interpret in the future, that is, a matter of learning to inherit.

This learning how to inherit, this opening up to the radically inherited nature of all genuine knowledge, traverses, in a variety of tonalities, Benjamin's corpus as a whole. As early as 6 September 1917, in a letter to Gershom Scholem, Benjamin insists that 'tradition is the medium in which the person who is learning continually transforms himself into the person who is teaching [*die Tradition ist das Medium in dem sich kontinuierlich der Lernende in den Lehrenden verwandelt*].' He stresses the ways in which an intellectual heir who 'encompasses the tradition in his own way makes it communicable by teaching. Knowledge becomes transmittable only for the person who has understood his knowledge as something that has been transmitted. He becomes free in an unprecedented way [*auf seine Weise die Tradition umfaßt und lehrend mitteilbar macht. Wer sein Wissen als überliefertes begriffen hat, in dem allein wird es überlieferbar, er wird in unerhörter Weise frei*].'[8] There can be no inheriting of a tradition without a perpetual transformation, in which the one who receives ('der Lernende') also becomes the one who passes on ('der Lehrende') – but one cannot have anything to pass on without first having struggled to receive it and to open up to its challenge. The task, as Benjamin tells us, is to grasp that the archive of all knowledge one might believe oneself to possess comes from an elsewhere. That is, this knowledge is an inherited tradition to which one chooses to relate in a singular and unprogrammable way. Indeed, there can be no *Überlieferbarkeit* of an intellectual tradition, no possibility for a heritage to be transmitted or handed down, without first wrestling with the implications of its very status *as* inheritance and transmission.

When Benjamin suggests that a certain experience of freedom suffuses this moment of grasping (*begreifen*), he qualifies it with the adverb 'unerhört', speaking of an experience of being 'in unerhörter Weise frei', being free in an unprecedented, or, more literally, an *unheard-of* way. This radical experience of freedom differs from any expected or more familiar notions of freedom in that it is predicated upon an understanding of knowledge as a matter of inherited transmission (*Überlieferung*) and transmissibility (*Überlieferbarkeit*). The freedom prompted by this particular knowledge about the transmitted, inherited status of all knowledge unfolds on the level of the uncontainable, the caesura that interrupts expected ways of relating to the concept and experience of freedom. It is no accident that Benjamin uses the word 'unerhört' in this context because, in addition to signifying something unprecedented, it also means 'scandalous' or 'outrageous'. The freedom that attends to the act of inheriting – the act of grasping (*begreifen*) knowledge as a mode of transmission and reception – also is a matter of scandal and outrage, since it cannot fully conform to established conventions, authorized procedures or legal norms for the inheritance of a legacy. What is 'unerhört' about the freedom that is at stake here is precisely the manner in which such freedom allows for unexpected, previously unknown modes of relating to the inherited knowledge or the transmitted legacy. The experience of the heir as the one who both receives and transmits a tradition is marked by a freedom that is conscious of its un-freedom (as it relates and answers to what came before it) *and* that affirms its own status as freedom precisely by striving to discover how to relate to the tradition in a new and singular way.

In Nietzsche's *Thus Spoke Zarathustra*, one of Benjamin's abiding intertexts, the always-recalcitrant act of inheriting-reading is explicitly thematized in the context of a thinking of genealogy. We find the following remark in the section 'On the Bestowing Virtue [*Von der schenkenden Tugend*]': 'Alas, much ignorance and error have become embodied in us! Not only the reason of millennia— their madness too breaks out in us [*auch ihr Wahnsinn bricht an uns aus*]. It is dangerous to be an heir [*Gefährlich ist es, Erbe zu sein*]'.[9] The target of Nietzsche's critique of reason is not merely the way in which certain aberrations from an otherwise triumphant march of reason deserve to be singled out for criticism and correction. On the contrary, Zarathustra's insight is precisely that the inheritance of an intellectual legacy is touched by the ever-present danger of inheriting a certain 'madness [*Wahnsinn*]' along with it, sometimes even instead of it. This danger can hardly be circumvented by means of the intellectual tools supplied by the inheritance itself. The opposite is the case: the tools themselves may even *be* the danger. For Nietzsche, the irreducible danger of being an heir is condensed in Zarathustra's consideration of death and even suicide in connection with the inheritance: 'Whoever has a goal and an heir [*Wer ein Ziel hat und einen Erben*] wants death at the right time for his goal and heir. And out of reverence for his goal and heir he will no longer hang withered wreaths in the sanctuary of life'.[10] Yet what would be 'the right time' with regard to a targeted goal and a recognized heir? When is the hour of the heir? And what kind of a goal connects the one who departs with the figure of his heir? If it is dangerous to be an heir, as

Nietzsche emphasizes, we are placed in the realm of a legacy in which we are constantly called upon to consider these questions anew, for they are forever intertwined with the concept and the experience of an intellectual inheritance itself.

In the act of receiving a legacy, the force of an intellectual inheritance may not always be distinguishable from its own weakness. From the perspective of the heir, it is not necessarily decidable in advance whether it is the strength or rather the weakness of an inheritance that is to be considered the stronger or more decisive force in one's relation to a legacy. As Jacques Derrida suggests in alluding to Benjamin's 'Theses on the Philosophy of History', both 'Nietzsche and Benjamin have encouraged us to have doubts on this score, each in his own way, and especially the latter when he associated "historical materialism" with the inheritance, precisely, of some "weak messianic force".'[11] As Derrida reminds us, one 'never inherits without coming to terms with [*s'expliquer avec*] some specter, and therefore with more than one specter.'[12] This perpetual coming-to-terms is the particular form that our haunting engagement with spectrality, our ghostly conversation with the dead, assumes. The condition of possibility for this spectral engagement with an inheritance is the legacy's resistance to transparency and understandability. 'If the readability of a legacy were given, natural, transparent, univocal [*Si la lisibilité d'un legs était donnée, naturelle, transparente, univoque*],' Derrida suggests, 'if it did not call for and at the same time defy interpretation, we would never have anything to inherit from it [*si elle n'appelait et ne défiait en même temps l'interprétation, on n'aurait jamais à en hériter*].' He continues: 'We would be affected by it as by a cause—natural or genetic. One always inherits from a secret—which says "read me, will you ever be able to do so?"'[13] Inheriting means inheriting from a secret, that is, from a language that exposes just enough of itself to be recognized *as* language, but that does not provide the tools with which to make sense of it. Its reading remains necessary but always also eludes closure.

The premise of the essays brought together in this book is that *to inherit* means *to interpret*. The legacy that is handed down to us can hardly be a matter of stable appropriation but rather exposes us to the difficulty of showing ourselves as responsible heirs to something that both beckons and resists us. The outcome of an act of inheriting can never be the assured recuperation of a loss or its sublation into a form of redemption. It may be tempting to take Benjamin's occasional mobilization of the tropes of redemption and recuperation at face value, as is done in some areas of Benjamin studies. Even a careful, erudite and redoubtable scholar of Benjamin such as Stéphane Mosès holds this optimistic view. 'As for Benjamin,' he tells us, 'he proposed the vision of a history in which nothing is sacrificed, nothing is lost forever. If each moment of the past can be reactualized, replayed under other conditions on a new stage, nothing in human history is irreparable.' From this perspective, 'the correction of the errors of the past' remains a permanent possibility.[14] But such an inter-pretation ultimately would amount to ascribing a Hegelian point of view to Benjamin that he does not share. For the Hegelian dialectical system, as memorably outlined in the *Phenomenology of Spirit*, in the end nothing really is lost because it can and will be reinscribed, in sublated form, in the progression of the dialectic itself. Each loss is only a loss for the time being – after all, its sublation and reinte-gration into the movement of *Geist* will be its conceptual redemption. While one might argue that there is a certain inability to mourn within the logic of Hegel's system, such is not the case in the world of Benjamin. Even – and, indeed, especially – in the act of inheriting, there can be no assured recuperation, no assumed overcoming of sacrifice. Instead, the act of inheriting is intricately bound up with the permanent possibility of absolute failure, radical loss, uncircum-ventable finitude and inconsolable mourning.

This permanent possibility also accounts for why Benjamin thinks the relation between *Erbe* and *Rettung* (recuperation, rescue, redemption, salvation) as a mode of conceptual labour along the double axis of promise and failure rather than as a triumphant accomplishment.[15] In the *Arcades Project*, for instance, Benjamin writes: 'From what are phenomena rescued? Not only, and not in the main, from the disrepute and the disregard into which they have fallen, but from the catastrophe that is presented very often by a certain means of their transmission [*Überlieferung*], their "appreciation as heritage or inheritance [*Würdigung als Erbe*]"—They are rescued through the exhibition of the crack [*Sprung*] within them.— There is a transmission that is catastrophe.'[16] If the inheritance of a phenomenon entails learning to relate to an *Erbe* in a way that is not merely a catastrophic handing-down, then the heir must attend to the crack or fissure [*Sprung*] that traverses what is to be inherited. For Benjamin, a catastrophic form of receiving and transmitting an inheritance occurs when the stability and self-identity of the inheritance is taken for granted, that is, when an heir is deaf to the specific and highly instructive ways in which the phenomenon, entity or archive to be inherited resists appropriation. To 'rescue' a phenomenon in the Benjaminian sense means to inherit it as the irreducible enigma that it is – and to attempt to interpret it always one more time. What remains in this particular form of rescuing is an interminable resistance to closure and completion, in other words, the never-ending act of inheriting.

Another way to put it is to say that what remains in Benjamin, the great thinker of the ruin and of what lives on in fragmented, disfigured form, are certain remains of inheriting. Yet Benjamin's remains remain to be seen, are yet to be received as a heritage always anew. In 'Remains to be Seen', the philosopher Stanley Cavell reflects on Benjamin and the *Arcades Project* by asking: 'Why (according to what allegories) make a work that cannot be read through? Perhaps to remind the reader that his and her work must perpetually find its own end. Why make a work that cannot be written to an end?

Perhaps to remind the writer of a reason to suffer awakening without end.'[17] Benjamin's texts do not promise closure and mastery, but rather – precisely by suffering awakening without end – they invite, even provoke, future acts of receiving the remains of a heritage. Reading and writing no longer conform to a model of communication or 'content-sharing', as one says in our digital age, but rather to the implications of the insight that, as Benjamin puts it, 'the Now of recognizability bears to the highest degree the stamp of that critical, dangerous moment that lies at the ground of all reading'.[18]

The critical, dangerous moment of reading that Benjamin evokes is not to be taken lightly – or 'merely' figuratively. Benjamin's singular modes of argumentation and apodictic writerly style have always caused his readers difficulty – and not all readers have been willing to commit themselves to the singular labour of inheriting that his texts require. Indeed, the density and originality of his thinking have worked to turn some readers into non-readers, who claim that, almost like Kafka's man from the country in the doorkeeper episode 'Before the Law', they can find no entry into his thought at all. When Benjamin attempted to secure the right to teach in the German university system with his *Habilitation* on the German Baroque mourning play – the rejection of which prevented him from embarking on an academic career in Germany even before such a possibility was negated by the National Socialists' takeover – the referee who had received the task of evaluating the work resisted Benjamin's study without ever actually engaging it. As the neo-Kantian philosopher Hans Cornelius wrote in his official report to the University of Frankfurt on 7 July 1925, sealing the book's fate: 'Dr. Benjamin's work, whose content as it relates to the study of art I have been asked to assess, is exceedingly difficult to read. A lot of words are used for which the author does not find it necessary to elucidate their sense, but which either have no commonly accepted meaning at all or which, when they are understood according to their usual meaning, yield no clear sense in the context in which they are employed.' Cornelius continues by relating that he, upon realizing his predicament, asked Benjamin for a concise summary of the *Trauerspiel* book, a request with which the latter complied. However, Cornelius claims, 'once again I did not succeed in understanding these elucidations'.[19] He comes to the conclusion that Benjamin, with his 'unintelligible manner of expression [*unverständliche Ausdrucksweise*], which must, after all, be interpreted as a sign of a substantive lack of clarity [*die doch wohl als Zeichen sachlicher Unklarheit gedeutet werden muß*], can be no guide or leader to students in this field [*kein Führer auf diesem Gebiet sein kann*]'.[20] Yes, one might say, Benjamin is no *Führer*. Leaving aside Cornelius' tendentious refusal to engage with Benjamin's thought on even the most basic level, it would be instructive to ask how our perspective on Benjamin's work would change if the core of Cornelius' criticism – that Benjamin uses words and concepts in a way that is not coextensive with their quotidian usage or that refunctionalizes them without fully explaining the terms of their refunctionalization – were seen not as an obstacle to be overcome on the way to the (quite possibly reactionary) dreamland of absolute transparency and clarity but rather were understood precisely as that which makes it possible to inherit Benjamin's provocative work in the first place. That is to say, what if the lack of conformity to an alleged commonplace and agreed-upon usage – a conformity which would, after all, leave nothing to interpret, nothing still in need of under-standing – were a necessary precondition for the act of innovative, rigorous, open-ended reading and, therefore, *inheriting*? Could not the very terms of Cornelius' criticism then be seen as marking the particular rigour, beauty and afterlife of Benjamin's words and works, that is, the Benjaminian archive as such? The present study hopes to keep this possibility alive.

The chapters that follow can be read sequentially or individually, as they each maintain a specific, self-contained focus on a key aspect of Benjamin's thinking, rather than unfolding in a linear manner a prescriptive proposition about how to inherit Benjamin today. The next chapter, Chapter 2, engages the question of inheritance through a consideration of Benjamin's 1934 Kafka essay, focusing on the concept of *Erbsünde*, or original sin. Chapter 3 takes up the discussion of Benjamin's engagement with a specific theological concept in the previous chapter by considering the category of theology in Benjamin's work more broadly. While Chapters 2 and 3 focus on the thinking of inheritance as it relates to theological concerns, Chapter 4 shifts our attention to the ways in which Benjamin inherits the category of critique in relation to the question of 'the thing'. This conjunction also connects Benjamin to Heidegger, another inheritor of the concepts of critique and the thing, even as their respective acts of inheriting separate the two thinkers from each other. Chapter 5, in turn, considers Benjamin's inheritance of formal (Kantian) and genealogical (Nietzschean) modes of analysing the work of art in the orbit of his aesthetic theory. Finally, Chapter 6, a miniature on time and photography after (that is, both following and in the manner of) Benjamin, presents a parting meditation on what it might mean to inherit time in the space of the image. To conclude this book on Benjamin and the question of inheritance with a reflection on time and the image of time is especially fitting because, for Benjamin, there can be no thinking of genealogy, no historicity, no tradition and, by extension, no inheritance that does not confront anew the question of time – and of going, or refusing to go, with time – whenever it seeks to provide an image of itself.

Collectively, then, these chapters conspire to yield a critical *constellation*, to mobilize one of Benjamin's own privileged tropes, that illuminates, from subtly shifting vantage points, a heterogeneous yet related network of concerns about the inheritance of the Benjaminian archive and its legacy. On the far side of systematicity and closure, the Benjaminian constellation formed by the chapters is attuned to the temporally and genealogically mediated view of inheritance. The time of inheritance, like Benjamin's time of history itself, is infinite and open, that is, unfulfilled and therefore radically other-directed. Future readings and reinterpretations will be called upon not only to invent new ways of inheriting the dispersed shards, fragments and ruins of Benjamin's intellectual project; they will also struggle to re-inherit his inexhaustible sentences and images in as-yet-unknown ways that would do justice to the unsettling yet necessary incompleteness of every historically inscribed act of inheriting a refractory legacy. These new forms of inheriting and their attendant acts of close rhetorical reading will wish to show themselves receptive both to the demand for slowness, care and circumspection and to the irrepressible political urgency that suffuses Benjamin's image, in his essay on Surrealism, of the historical alarm clock that rings, not occasionally, but for sixty seconds every minute.

Erbsünde: A Note on Paradoxical Inheritance in Benjamin's Kafka Essay

One encounters a strangely fascinating conceptual resistance when reading Walter Benjamin's sentences, an often unarticulated or absent figure of an elsewhere that is seldom set forth explicitly. They are, one senses, 'about' what they seem to be about, and yet always also about something else, a subterranean network that remains unnamed, something whose thinkability often appears indebted to its very refusal to name. One way of engaging this elsewhere in Benjamin's writerly corpus is to attend to the numerous figures of non-synchronicity, temporal rupture, living on and lateness that permeate his words, figures and thoughts.[1] It may be here, rather than in his more 'canonical' pronouncements – that is, the orthodox core of Benjamin's writings that is so central to the critical field today – that certain unexpected potentialities of his intellectual archive remain to be found.

Among the themes that comprise what might be termed the language and logic of a certain 'afterness' in Benjamin's thinking, the problem of intellectual and experiential inheritance ('Erbe' or 'Erbschaft') stands out. It is no accident that, in his 1937 essay on the cultural historian Eduard Fuchs, Benjamin refers to 'the notion of inheritance that also is significant once again today [*Begriff des Erbes, der auch heute wieder seine Bedeutung hat*]'.[2] To be sure, Benjamin here is thinking of the discourses of his time – among other things, the problem of inheritance in the afterlife of historical materialism as developed by Marx, Engels and their successors, and the attendant question – debated by Georg Lukács, Ernst Bloch, Hanns Eisler and others – as to how to relate to a cultural and intellectual inheritance that has been tainted by political appropriations and ideological deformations.[3] Yet at the same time, a more general engagement with the question of intellectual inheritance and its difficulties also is at stake. Benjamin wishes to begin to think inheritance *as* inheritance, that is, as a fundamental theoretical problem that leaves no part of an intellectual or artistic project, and indeed no being-in-the-world, untouched.

In what follows, I wish to read a single passage from Benjamin's 1934 essay on Kafka, first published in the *Jüdische Rundschau* under the title 'Franz Kafka. Zur zehnten Wiederkehr seines Todestages' ('Franz Kafka: On the Tenth Anniversary of His Death'), with the question of inheritance in mind. This essay belongs to Benjamin's complex and far-reaching network of engagements with the work of Kafka, which spans more than a decade. His texts include a review of Max Brod's Kafka biography, the lecture 'Franz Kafka: Beim Bau der Chinesischen Mauer', various paralipomena, notes and sketches, as well as extensive epistolary exchanges on the topic of Kafka with his central intellectual interlocutors, Gershom Scholem, Theodor W. Adorno, Werner Kraft, Bertolt Brecht and others.[4] Among the first-generation Frankfurt School thinker's reception of Kafka, Benjamin's essay is genealogically situated between his friend Siegfried Kracauer's 1931 essay 'Franz Kafka' published in the *Frankfurter Zeitung* and Adorno's later essay, begun in 1942 and first published in 1953 in *Die Neue Rundschau*, 'Notes on Kafka [*Aufzeichnungen zu Kafka*]'.[5] In the scholarly literature, Benjamin's Kafka essay has been appropriately understood as marking the transition from Benjamin's early concerns with specifically literary and formal philosophical problems to the seemingly more cultural, historical and materialist concerns that delimit the theory of modernity as it would emerge in the *Arcades*

Project – a conceptual shift, however, that in the Kafka essay remains suggestively incomplete at best.[6] And from the perspective of the literature on Kafka, Benjamin's essay has often been seen as a paradigmatic test case for a reading of Kafka that emphasizes the writer's engagement with Judaism and the multiple Jewish legacies of his writing, an interpretative trajectory whose first proponent, however superficially, was Kafka's friend and literary executor, Brod.[7] But my aim here is not to add to these well-known discussions; I have in mind something rather more modest and partial. It is my wager that learning how to read the language and logic of a single Benjaminian passage will help us learn how to inherit the strange singularity and idiomaticity of his movements of thought and writing more generally. In so doing, it will behove us to resist the temptation to reduce Benjamin's language merely to this or that propositional content, a content that would be deaf to its own appearance in a particular linguistic formulation and, by extension, indifferent to the unreliable workings of language as such.

The passage in question is seldom remarked upon by Benjamin's commentators. This may be, in part, because the paratactical composition and conceptual elusiveness of the Kafka essay can seem like a refusal on the part of Benjamin to engage in textual exegesis at all. And so, for readers such as the literary critic Robert Alter – who are perhaps too affirmatively convinced that Benjamin, along with Kafka and Scholem, 'perceived a sustaining power of visionary truth and an authenticity in Jewish tradition while fearing that this truth and this authenticity might no longer be accessible to them' – what appears 'odd' in 'Benjamin's relation to exegesis is that he speculated about it, contemplated it as an ideal of writing and cognition, without ever quite getting around to practicing it.'[8] Benjamin's 'remarkable essays on Kafka' and others, in Alter's view, 'illustrate metaphysical speculations or historical generalizations' rather than 'set[ting] texts for exposition through commentary.'[9] But what if Benjamin's seeming refusal to translate the multiple vagaries of Kafka's text into the treacherously stable idiom of achieved hermeneutic certainty were not merely an oddity or a shortcoming but rather the very condition of possibility for any attempt to do justice to the complexity of the problems that are at stake? That is to say, what if Benjamin's way of remaining faithful to Kafka's uneasy inheritance, to Kafka *as* inheritance, consisted in his commitment to acknowledging as rigorously as possible the ways in which the questions that Kafka's texts pose – precisely in their own, idiomatic terms – coax into being modes of reflection that lead ever more deeply into the complexity of the problems they help us to articulate rather than calling for responses that would undo the questions by providing alleged answers? Allowing oneself to be led ever more deeply into a problem rather than wishing to be guided out of it would then figure as a particular mode of inheriting a textual legacy in which the relation to what is inherited remains open and free, that is, unforeclosed by an heir's premature sense of ownership and seamless appropriation.

This refractory and resistant form of inheritance is staged in the first of the four parts of Benjamin's Kafka essay, subtitled 'Potemkin'. In the context of the ever-shifting constellation of reason, paternity and justice in Kafka, Benjamin writes:

> Der Vater, der der Strafende ist, ist zugleich auch der Ankläger. Die Sünde, deren er den Sohn bezichtigt, scheint eine Art Erbsünde zu sein. Denn wen trifft die Bestimmung, welche Kafka von ihr gegeben hat, mehr als den Sohn: 'Die Erbsünde, das alte Unrecht, das der Mensch begangen hat, besteht in dem Vorwurf, den der Mensch macht und von dem er nicht abläßt, daß ihm ein Unrecht geschehen ist, daß an ihm die Erbsünde begangen wurde.' Wer aber wird dieser Erbsünde—der Sünde einen Erben gemacht zu haben—bezichtigt wenn nicht der Vater durch den Sohn? Somit wäre der Sündige der Sohn. Nicht aber darf man aus dem Satze Kafkas schließen, daß die Bezichtigung sündig sei, weil falsch. Nirgends steht bei Kafka, daß sie zu Unrecht erfolgt.[10]

The published English translation of the text renders this passage as follows:

> Fathers punish, but they are at the same time accusers. The sin of which they accuse their sons seems to be a kind of original sin. The definition of it which Kafka has given applies to the sons more than to anyone else: 'Original sin, the old injustice committed by man, consists in the complaint unceasingly made by man that he has been the victim of an injustice, the victim of original sin.' But who is accused of this inherited sin—the sin of having produced an heir—if not the father by the son? Accordingly, the son would be the sinner. But one must not conclude from Kafka's definition that the accusation is sinful because it is false. Nowhere does Kafka say that it is made wrongfully.[11]

Let us begin to approach this immensely rich passage by way of some linguistic observations. In Benjamin's original German, 'der Vater' is singular, whereas in the published English translation, this singular noun turns into a plural one, 'Fathers'. But can there ever be more than one father? Who or what can have more than one father, the One? Who or what would authorize the transition from the one to the many? What are the conditions of the pluralized father? Likewise, Benjamin's 'der Sohn', singular, is rendered as 'sons', plural. This translation – not only between languages but also between numbers – is justified to the extent that it is possible in the German idiom to employ a singular noun to speak of a plural concept, especially when what is at stake is the universality of a general structure or concept. The locutions 'Der Vater' and 'der Sohn' therefore act as a stand-in for an implicit act performed by 'die Väter' and 'die Söhne', fathers and sons as such. Yet the singular designations of 'der Vater' and 'der Sohn' persist even in the universal locution, so that what survives within the general filial structure is precisely the idiomatic singularity of this particular father (Kafka's) and this particular son (Kafka himself), a singularity that may at times resist being subsumed under the universalizing category, because it serves as an alleged example of it. Benjamin's specific hovering between singularity and universality here also pays homage to Kafka's own locution in his well-known *Brief an den Vater* (1919), the long plaintive reckoning he addresses to his father, which performs its own kind of hovering, that between 'der Vater' as the more objectified 'the father' and 'der Vater' specified and personalized as 'my father'. While the title of that text is usually translated as *Letter to His Father*, the translation can be misleading as it introduces the determinacy of a distance and a form of relation that is not to be found in Kafka's own language, a language that keeps suspended the relation between distance and proximity, the singularity of *this* particular father here and the exigencies of *that* father over there, which may or may not be simply 'his' or even 'mine'.[12] Kafka exploits the idiomatic German way of indicating one's proprietorial relationship to something or someone by employing the definite article 'an *den*' rather than the possessive pronoun 'an *meinen*'; in so doing he situates his text precisely on the fence between an apostrophe directed at his father and one directed at fathers and fatherhood as such.

Benjamin's and Kafka's indeterminate hovering between singularity and universality is erased in the English translation, even though the latter is technically not incorrect. One might say that the English translation of 'der Vater' and 'der Sohn' inherits Benjamin's German precisely in a manner that trips over the internal resistance that its inheritance harbours. As such, it performs something of the aporetic moment of inheriting that is at stake in the passage itself, becoming – against its own intention, as it were – a successful failure. To put it in an epigrammatically condensed way: It refuses, or fails, to fail *merely* unsuccessfully, undialectically.

The passage on *Erbsünde* that Benjamin quotes from Kafka appears as an entry dated 15 November 1920 in notebook 12 of Kafka's *Tagebücher*, his diaries. It is also included in the prose collection *Beim Bau der chinesischen Mauer*.[13] We might note, attending to a cross-linguistic echo, that the text in which Kafka's passage appears sometimes is published under the title 'Er' ('He'), in which the phonically indistinguishable German 'Er' and English 'heir' become, as it were, homophonic heterographs.[14] The particular relation that, in Benjamin's reading of Kafka, connects father and son is given the name 'Erbsünde'. While the English translation provides the correct standard equivalent from the Biblical tradition, 'original sin', different conceptualizations are implicitly operative in the German and the English terms. 'Original sin', like its German relatives 'Ursünde' and 'Sündenfall', emphasizes an originary Fall, a departure from a previous course or state of affairs, which subsequently led to a fallen, that is, postlapsarian world. Its reference is to the original sin narrated in the Book of Genesis – succumbing to the snake's temptation to eat a fruit from the Tree of Knowledge of Good and Evil in defiance of God's prohibition – which then becomes the primordial sin upon which all subsequent forms of sin are based.

This moment of original sin, and especially its implications for language as such, always attracted Benjamin. For instance, in his 1916 essay on the philosophy of language, 'On Language as Such and on the Language of Man', he evokes original sin, the 'Sündenfall', in terms of a double structure of decline and generativity in which 'the Fall marks the birth hour of the *human word* [*der Sündenfall ist die Geburtsstunde des menschlichen Wortes*], in which name no longer lives intact and which has stepped out of name-language, the language of knowledge'. According to the terms of the inheritance handed down by this scene of the Fall, 'after the promise of the snake', the 'word must communicate *something* (other than itself)'.[15] The 'Sündenfall' thus forces an excessive relationship between word and world – in the sense that the word is now forced to have a referential, rather than purely self-referential function – at the same time that it inaugurates the tradition of human language itself, that is, founds a legacy in which the human will be called upon to locate himself in the language into which he is always already born and to search for himself in a world that always already precedes him and with whose ineluctable before-ness he must constantly strive to come to terms.

Yet in the specific passage from the 1934 Kafka essay, the word in question is not 'Sündenfall' but, precisely, 'Erbsünde'. The linguistic particularity of the German term that both Benjamin and Kafka employ here, which should be read carefully in its two parts as *Erb-sünde*, shifts the emphasis from an originary act itself to the *transmission* and *legacy* of that act. Taken literally, *Erb-sünde* means 'inheritance sin', ambivalently naming *both* the sin that is inherited *and* the sin of inheriting itself, that is, inheritance as sin. *Erbsünde* sets into motion an inheritance that becomes tradition, even if – or precisely when – its legacy is poisoned or has fallen ill. Seen from this perspective, it is no accident that Benjamin, in his long essay-letter about Kafka to Scholem on 12 June 1938, avers that 'Kafka's work presents a sickness of tradition [*Kafkas Werk stellt eine Erkrankung der Tradition dar*]' and, as such, concerns itself over and over again with the question of 'transmissability [*Tradierbarkeit*]'.[16] What is at stake is the very ability of something to be turned into a tradition, handed down, received by an heir who, in turn, will perpetuate it by wrestling with it, interpreting it and making it the touchstone of his own answerability to the difficulty of what has come before.

It is worth noting that when Benjamin moves from a more circumscribed experience of tradition in Kafka's work to the larger questions of legacy and transmissability that arise from it, he employs the term 'Tradierbarkeit' rather than merely 'Tradition'. As Samuel Weber has demonstrated – without actually discussing the specific term 'Tradierbarkeit' – Benjamin's unusual strategy of forming a large number of nouns by adding the suffix '-barkeit' ('-ability') can be read as something more than a stylistic idiosyncrasy. By creating an extensive number of nouns formed with the suffix '-barkeit' in key moments of his texts – with such formations as

'Reproduzierbarkeit' (reproducibility), 'Übersetzbarkeit' (translatability) or 'Kritisierbarkeit' (criticizability) among the most prominent
– Benjamin works to emphasize possibility, capacity and potentiality, rather than achieved or existing reality.[17] Whether something
is eventually turned into an existing reality often is secondary
in Benjamin's thought to a consideration of the ways in which
something maintains its pure potential, its future-directed capacity.
An achieved – 'merely' achieved – reality or new state of affairs
could even be thought to stand in the way of the open-ended and
unfulfilled nature of pure possibility, a potentiality that is encoded
in all the '-barkeiten' that populate the orbit of Benjamin's thought.
In the case of the problem of 'Tradierbarkeit' in Kafka, we might say
that Benjamin focuses his attention not exclusively on the alleged
content of this or that tradition but rather on that content's capacity
to be handed down. In other words, his focus is on the way in which
a tradition becomes visible and inheritable *as* tradition. From this
perspective, the 'Tradierbarkeit' of a legacy would seem to be inextricably linked to a word that does not appear in Benjamin's lexicon but
whose logic and implications are nevertheless present everywhere,
that is, 'Erbbarkeit' (inheritability).

If a tradition has fallen ill – thereby evoking questions of legacy,
genealogy, transmission and legibility anew and under an altered sign
– then specific elements that inhabit this tradition would have to be
reread in light of the shifting relations among those elements within
the space and time of the legacy in which they occur. It is no different
in the particular relation of the legacy or tradition connecting
father and son. After all, it, too, is struck in Kafka by a particular
Erkrankung. Between father and son there obtains a paradoxical
relation, one mediated by the inheritance of an *Erbsünde*. The father,
who enacts the double role of plaintiff and punisher, accuses the son
of an *Erbsünde* – here, the very sin of producing an *Erbe*, an heir –
even though he himself is the originator of that sin, and therefore

the one who passes on the legacy of an inheritance. But according to Kafka's logic of inheritance, the *Erbsünde* consists not in having committed an original sin but rather in assuming that a sin has been committed against one, that is, that a self has suffered an injustice that has been inflicted upon it. This particular form of injustice is itself the *Erbsünde* because it mistakes the tacit genealogy of a perceived injustice with its interpretation (or misinterpretation) as a matter of lived experience. For Benjamin, if this paradoxical logic of inheritance can be thought in the context of the relation between father and son, then the one who has committed the *Erbsünde* is in fact the son, not the father ('Somit wäre der Sündige der Sohn'). The sin would then consist in having inherited a misinterpretation of one's own suffering and of having persisted in that misinterpretation. The precise terms of *Erbsünde* in Benjamin's reading of Kafka could then be formalized as follows: *die Sünde geerbt zu haben* (to have inherited sin) becomes *die Sünde, geerbt zu haben* (the sin of having inherited), a fundamental difference marked in German by the presence or absence of a mere comma.

It is important to note that within the conceptual and theological history of *Erbsünde* one of the most central debates has been over the question of culpability and guilt. If the inherited sin can be understood merely as an un-asked-for, unwanted affliction that seizes a subject from elsewhere – another context that always already precedes and therefore exculpates a guilt-inheriting self – then the question of responsibility and the notion of freedom (in relation to choosing or not choosing to relate to this guilt in a particular way) can hardly be located in any normative realm of individual ethics.[18] For the term *Erbsünde*, which was first introduced into German as an interpretation of the Latin *peccatum originale* by the influential late-medieval German-language preacher Johann Geiler von Kaysersberg and subsequently was firmly established in the German language by Luther, has always fluctuated between an assignment of guilt to the subject and the subject's implicit exoneration owing to its unintentional affliction by something for something which predates it and for which it cannot assume guilt. There have been thinkers of *Erbsünde*, such as Augustine, who have attempted to mediate the tension between a guilt that can be assumed due to free choice and a guilt that cannot be assumed because the act that caused the original sin stands in a merely derivate relationship to a conscious subject who can contemplate this guilt. In the wake of the reflections by Augustine and later by Luther, the particular nature of the *Schuld* (a word which in German means both debt and guilt) that is inscribed in *Erbsünde* has continued to occupy thinkers into modernity. The logic and implications of *Erbsünde* have evoked sustained reflections in thinkers as variegated as Kant, Hegel, Kierkegaard, Schleiermacher and Schopenhauer, among others.[19]

In excess of particular genealogical formulations, certain structures always traverse the concept of *Erbsünde* as such. The question of the *Erbsünde* that orients the relation between the one who passes on an inheritance, the inheritance itself, and the inheritor is inscribed in the logic of a law, even the lawness of the law, whose meaning remains opaque. As Jacques Derrida demonstrates in his sustained 1982 London lecture on Kafka's 'Before the Law' – a short parable that was included in *The Trial* but that Kafka also decided to publish separately, that is, 'before' (in advance of and in view of) the law that the later novel would impose on it, as it were – the experience of the so-called man from the country of not being allowed entrance into the law stages a certain failure of reading. The law in question, which cannot be reduced to a specific law of a natural, ethical, institutional, political, etc. nature, signifies the law as law, the lawness of the law as such. The problem is not that the doorkeeper maliciously prevents the man from the country from entering the law. Rather, the man himself fails as a careful reader, that is, he is incapable of grasping that a law cannot be entered at all, that it refuses – even while allowing indirect glimpses of itself – to grant access to itself, perpetually manifesting the specific ways in which it remains inaccessible. The law, in the idiom of Kafka's literary rendition of it, is marked by a double imperative: it perpetually invites and provokes readings that necessarily remain impossible. That is, our readings of the law are both required and foreclosed.[20] Inheriting the law would, by extension, always also have to confront the double provocation of this necessity and this impossibility, along with the complex histories of reading and the contested interpretations to which they have given rise.

To attempt to inherit Benjamin inheriting Kafka inheriting the 'inheritance sin', it is imperative to become attuned to how the difficulty and unreadability of the law operate upon any such inheritance. Rodolphe Gasché's reading of Benjamin's essay on Kafka in relation to the double heritage of Judaism and Hellenism underscores the particular ways in which, for Benjamin, the notion of the law as such does not provide access to the significance and trajectory of Kafka's writings. It is instructive to note that Benjamin, in his letter to Scholem dated 11 August 1934, singles out the law as the *toten Punkt*, or dead point, in any interpretation of Kafka: 'I consider Kafka's perpetual insistence upon the law to be the dead point of his work, by which I only wish to say that, as far as interpretation goes, it does not seem to be moveable from precisely that point [*Kafkas stetes Drängen nach dem Gesetz halte ich für den toten Punkt seines Werkes, womit ich nur sagen will, daß es grade von ihm aus interpretativ mir nicht zu bewegen scheint*].'[21] Commenting on the *Erbsünde* passage in Benjamin's Kafka essay, Gasché suggests that the 'sin which permeates this world inhibits all clear differentiation' and causes 'father and son' to 'appear intimately connected, and in solidarity with the fear that pervades all the orders on the nether or natural side of the world, that is, its procreational side.'[22] To further our grasp of the logic or non-logic of the law in Benjamin's reading of Kafka, Gasché reminds us of the following: The accusation of an injustice that has been brought against the father by the son, in Benjamin's words, is not 'sinful because it is false'. In fact, according to Benjamin, 'nowhere does Kafka say that [the accusation] is made wrongfully [*zu Unrecht*]'. These statements, as Gasché rightly emphasizes, do not necessarily mean that Benjamin 'contend[s] that the accusation is correct'. On the contrary, the 'old injustice, or rather, the old wrong, which pits father against son ... comes with the impossibility of deciding who has been wronged. The law of prehistory is not simply one of wrongs.' One may speak, by extension, of 'a law that inhibits the possibility of discriminating between right and wrong', a law that is 'constituted by the very impossibility of a clear decision – an impossibility by which this law perpetuates the order of wrong (*Unrecht*), thus also excluding the very possibility of justice (*Gerechtigkeit*)'.[23] This basic structure, one might say, is operative in heterogeneous modulations in all of Kafka's canonical texts, and especially in such works as *The Trial*, 'In the Penal Colony' and 'The Judgment'.

Yet there is another law at work in this logic, a law that pertains to legacy, tradition, reception – in short, what could be called the law of inheritance, or *Erbe*. Inheriting something, finding oneself the heir of a legacy one does not fully understand, requires opening up to the difficulty of that legacy, its suspension between legibility and illegibility. This act of inheriting also calls upon the heir to acknowledge that the difficulty of the inheritance itself, rather than the one who hands it down, is responsible for the burden it has placed upon the one who inherits. The uneasy, even ghostly task of inheriting is precisely to learn to confront, engage and ceaselessly interpret this burden, inviting the difficulty of the inheritance as inheritance, rather than attempting to circumvent it through a supposedly seamless act of appropriation. Just as Benjamin, through Kafka, in a move that on the surface appears paradoxical, suggests that the sin of the *Erbsünde* may not lie with the father but in actuality with the son who inherits the father's legacy, so the 'sin' of inheriting is to be negotiated not with a focus on the one who or that which bequeaths an inheritance, but rather with a focus on how the inheritor, as the recipient of a tradition that emanates from elsewhere, relates to that inheritance – that is, how well he learns to struggle with its competing meanings and unfathomable implications.

In the case of the *Erbsünde* that structures the relation between father and son in Kafka and that between Kafka and his heir Benjamin, what imposes itself on consciousness is not only a responsibility toward the ways in which the inheritance offers itself to interpretation while simultaneously withdrawing from it, but also a certain kind of orphanhood, a becoming-orphaned. The one who inherits becomes an orphan. This is so not only because an inheritance is typically bequeathed in the case of a parent's, guardian's or elder's prior death, but also because the price that is paid for inheriting something, including an intellectual or immaterial legacy, is to be thrown into the condition of having been left behind, a scene of departure and leave-taking, mourning, and the experience of becoming, literally or figuratively, orphaned. No inheritance without orphans. Indeed, the primal scene of the *Erbsünde*, which in the Biblical tradition is believed to have set into motion the perpetual sinfulness of humankind into which one is born, is inexorably tied to the scene of Adam and Eve's abandonment, the moment in which they are permanently expelled from the Garden of Eden by their creator.

It is striking to note, therefore, that the etymology of the German word 'Erbe' encrypts something of the history of this process of becoming an orphan.[24] The history of the semantically complex word 'Erbe' is inseparable from that of the orphan. The origin of the term, which can be documented in early Germanic and Celtic sources, in Old High German was 'erbi' and in Middle High German 'erbe', which is genetically related to the Gothic 'arbi' and the Old English 'ierfi'. It is primordially linked (the Duden etymology speaks of 'urverwandt') with the Old Irish 'orbe' and the Latin 'orbus', meaning 'robbed', the Greek 'orphanós' (orphaned) and Armenian 'orb' (orphan). These and related formations derive from the Indo-European root '*orbho-' (orphaned; orphan). Therefore, it can be argued that the original meaning of 'Erbe' is 'orphaned possession' or 'possession of the orphan'. In the orbit of this same etymological root one finds the ancestors of the German word for 'work', that is, 'Arbeit', which originally signified the 'hard physical labour of an orphaned child', and of the German word for 'poor', 'arm', which once signified 'orphaned'. If 'Erbe' is always suffused with a form of orphanhood, as the Indo-European '*orbho' suggests, then an inheritance can always also be thought as a form of becoming orphaned. What is passed on and what is inherited are always also orphaned goods.

But if the orphaned goods of an inheritance are associated with the hard labour of an orphan (the orphan's *Arbeit*), they also evoke the hard, slow, patient and questioning labour of reading, that is, the laborious process of opening up to receive the language and objects of the other who passes on a legacy. There can be no inheritance in the strong sense of the concept without this labour of orphanhood, without shouldering the burden of a rigorous reading and vigilant reinterpretation. To the extent that 'Erben' and 'Erbschaft' are etymologically linked to the labour (*Arbeit*) and poverty (*Armut*) of an orphaned child, who emerges as something akin to a serf, the moment of inheritance is touched, in its Sisyphean despair, by a certain mourning. It is no accident that the Old High German 'erbi' and the Middle High German 'erbe' are not only related to the Anglo-Saxon 'erbi' and Middle Low German 'erve' but, significantly, also to the Old Norse 'erfi', which names a funeral reception or commemoration of the departed. In the latter sense of 'erfi', an inheritance always also gathers around death and finitude, the unrepresentable experience of life as death-oriented and as resistant to full hermeneutic disclosure.

The history of language – at least in the German case of the 'Erbe' that is at stake in Benjamin's inheritance of Kafka and in their forms of thinking the question of inheritance – preserves something of the abiding interpenetration that is not usually visible on the surface but that forever joins an inheritance with a funeral reception, welding the work of mourning, even the hard labour or *Arbeit* of a rigorous textual encounter with a logic and a language that are seen only in their withdrawal and understood only as distant echoes of a time and a thinking that already are no more.

One of the many precepts that follow from assuming this perspective is that the son must learn to recognize himself as an inheritor in mourning who is called upon to engage the difficult labour of learning to read the inheritance; he must grasp, in other words, that the inheritance, far from being an appropriable possession, *is* precisely this mournful process of reading and interpreting. As such, the son is both son to his father and at the same time – in the moment of recognizing the demands placed upon him by the mournful inheritance and its perpetual and properly interminable interpretation – *also* an orphan. According to this logic, we might say that the son is always already an actual or future orphan, regardless of whether his father is in fact alive or dead. One way of glossing the *Erbsünde* that circulates through Kafka's language, as well as through Benjamin's inheritance of it, is to prepare the scene for an (albeit deferred) understanding, a distant intimation, of the orphanhood that the inheritance calls into being. Yet even this perceived ophanhood can never become a matter of mere possession. It can only be thought and shared to the extent that it refuses to be fully possessed, that is, to the extent that it eludes the illusions bestowed upon us by our often premature sense of ownership of this or that experience.

This way of thinking complicates our understanding of Brod's refusal to enact a particular mode of inheriting, that is, Kafka's testamentary wish to see his manuscripts destroyed after his death (a way of relating to Kafka's legacy to which Benjamin also devoted a short text from 1929, 'Kavaliersmoral').[25] The problem of inheritance emerges as a force field of differences and deferrals that is lodged at the core of the spectral logic and afterlife of a legacy. As these lines concerning inheritance are being written – that is, as they themselves perform a kind of inheritance of Benjamin inheriting Kafka – another date and another legacy subtly inscribe themselves. This is to say that the present lines will also have been written, almost unwittingly, in commemorative reflection on the death of a great inheritor of Benjamin and Kafka, Derrida. It is as if these lines, composed exactly one decade after the latter's passing, were subtitled, or subtitled themselves, 'Jacques Derrida: Zur zehnten Wiederkehr seines Todestages' ('Jacques Derrida: On the Tenth Anniversary [or: Return] of his Death'). For is it not Derrida who 'has always recognized' himself 'in the figure of the heir' and who reminds us that when it comes to an inheritance 'it is necessary to do everything to appropriate a past even though we know that it remains fundamentally inappropriable, whether it is a question of philosophical memory or the precedence of a language, a culture, and a filiation in general'?[26] For him, engaging with an inheritance 'means not simply accepting this heritage but relaunching it otherwise and keeping it alive. Not choosing it (since what characterizes a heritage is first of all that one does not choose it; it is what violently elects us), but choosing to keep it alive.'[27] If there is a 'tension internal to a heritage', and if 'our heritage assigns contradictory tasks to us (to receive and yet to choose, to welcome what comes before us and yet to reinterpret it, etc.), this is because it is a testimony to our finitude. Only a finite being inherits, and his finitude *obliges* him.'[28] Because no inheritance can be thought without finitude – a shared finitude that binds a self to the other – the thought of inheritance also must confront a double obligation: to the inheritance 'itself' – that is, its 'content' – and to the very finitude whose horizon first makes the act of inheriting possible.

The nature of this obligation is such that the heir of the inheritance is called upon to choose and thus also to exclude, to show himself responsible to the inheritance by learning to respond to it, answering to it in a singular way. Derrida explains:

> The concept of responsibility has no sense at all outside of an experience of inheritance … One is responsible before what comes before one but also before what is to come, and therefore *before oneself*. A double *before*, one that is also a debt, as when we say *devant ce qu'il doit*: *before* what he *ought to do* and *owing* what he *owes*, once and for all, the heir is doubly indebted. It is always a question of a sort of anachronism: to come before [*devancer*] in the name of what came before us, and to come before the name itself! To invent one's name, to sign otherwise, uniquely in each case but in the name of the name passed down, if that's possible![29]

Taking on an inheritance calls for assuming the enormous responsibility for a past that, in the moment of inheritance, is a matter of futurity, a non-saturated, non-completed time to come that is still to be invented. One finds oneself the heir of something that comes from elsewhere, a past that is no more, but in a manner that comes to collect a debt that one is not sure one can ever repay or even fully understand. The heir thus finds himself at the juncture of a history that has produced him and that propels him to reinterpret it without end in such a way as to be faithful to it and to betray it at the same time, to follow it, in the double sense of coming after it and accepting its precepts, precisely by not following it, rereading it, grafting it onto other commitments, unexpected concerns, situations and discourses.

The paradoxical inheritance that is named by the *Erbsünde* and that is passed on through the relation between father and son, or parent and orphan, cannot but confront the demand that it be read and reread, reinterpreted and thus reinherited always one more time. Following Benjamin inheriting Kafka means inviting the simultaneous necessity and impossibility of a legacy without attempting merely to disinherit the contingencies and resistances that such a tradition hands down to us. On the contrary, inheriting would mean receiving precisely the singular demand of an answerability for which there can be no stable ground and in which, as in Benjamin's radical assessment of postlapsarian modernity in the *Trauerspiel* book, the heir must confront the permanent threat posed by the insight that 'any person, any object, any relationship can mean absolutely anything else [*jede Person, jedwedes Ding, jedes Verhältnis kann ein beliebiges anderes bedeuten*]'.[30] It is here, in the space of this double possibility, forever linking the disclosure of meaning to its retreat, that a reluctant yet receptive heir may begin to receive the legacy of a future based on the unending interpretation of an inheritance that has not been decided once and for all, but instead remains always yet to come. To refuse the uneasy legacy of this openness would be to foreclose the act of inheriting itself. Indeed, it would constitute another kind of *Erbsünde*.

Benjamin's Blotting Paper: Writing and Erasing a Theological Figure of Thought

In idiomatic German, there is a term for the moment at which someone is asked an especially difficult, uncomfortable or probingly personal question, *die Gretchenfrage* ('the Gretchen-question'). The *Gretchenfrage* puts someone on the spot, wishing to elicit a revelation or even a confession from the one to whom the question has been posed. The questioner may wish to achieve clarity as to the other's intentions or, following a time of doubt or confusion, hope to gain access to the other's previously hidden views – especially in relation to contested matters of a religious, political, financial, ethical or sexual nature. Like so many modern German concepts and idioms, the *Gretchenfrage* can be traced back to Goethe's epic poem, the tragic drama *Faust*. In the first part of the tragedy, young Margarete, or Gretchen for short, responds to the increasingly intense romantic advances of the much older scholar and scientist Faust by inquiring of him: 'Nun sag, wie hast du's mit der Religion? Du bist ein herzlich guter Mann, allein ich glaub, du hälst nicht viel davon [Now say, where do you stand on religion? You are a dear good man, yet I believe you don't think much of it].'[1] In response to Gretchen's query, Faust equivocates with a philosophical meditation on the concept of religion and its place in an enlightened, secular and scientifically oriented age, leaving Gretchen consternated and ultimately unconvinced of his commitment to Christianity. To this day, as relationships deepen and evolve, Germans like to ask each other Gretchen-questions of all sorts. But the Ur-*Gretchenfrage* is still the question of religious and theological belief, as Faust's Gretchen originally advances it. Although his influential essay on Goethe does not directly concern *Faust* but rather the novel *Elective Affinities*, one of Goethe's most insightful interpreters, Walter Benjamin, was, like any educated German in the first part of the twentieth century, undoubtedly familiar with the *Gretchenfrage* and the famous scene in the garden of Gretchen's neighbour Marthe in which its dramatic staging takes place. Turning the critical telescope the other way, we might ask whether there is not also something like a *Gretchenfrage* in relation to Benjamin's own variegated corpus. In other words, to what extent are matters of religion and theology relevant, even unavoidable, in inheriting him today? In putting the *Gretchenfrage* to Benjamin in this way, we embark on a line of questioning that is not the same as that of Nietzsche, who, in his critique of German Idealism in *The Anti-Christ: A Curse on Christianity*, bitingly remarks that 'one only has to utter the word "Tübinger Stift" in order to comprehend *what* German philosophy is at bottom—a *perfidious* theology [*eine* hinterlistige *Theologie*]'.[2] Rather, our *Gretchenfrage* in this chapter, as a mode of inheriting Benjamin, interrogates a series of irreducibly theological investments, involvements, enactments, legacies and displacements that are lodged at the core of Benjamin's intellectual project.

For better or for worse, Benjamin is still best-known to a broad readership for his transformative commentary on the concept of the artwork in the age of its infinite mechanical reproducibility, his prescient views on the history and theory of photography, his visionary media-theoretical writings, his cultural analyses of the logic of the commodity and his meditations on the dialectically vexed experience of modernity itself. At the same time, the fact that his texts are traversed by the language of theologically inflected motifs – from the concept of Now-Time to the question of redemption, from the idea of a 'weak messianic power' to the figure of the angel in his theses on the philosophy of history, from his mobilization of the Greek *apokatastasis* (the bringing back of all) to his use of terms from Jewish mysticism, from his notions of remembrance and commemoration, through a critique of capitalism as religion, to his poignant figures of hope – cannot be missed by readers who acquaint themselves with a broad cross-section of his writings. Moreover, Benjamin's early intellectual formation is known to have been significantly influenced not only by his close friend Gershom Scholem, who invented modern Jewish Studies, but also by the theologically suffused liberationist utopianism of Ernst Bloch, the redemptive theology of Franz Rosenzweig and even the political theology of the conservative legal theorist Carl Schmitt.

Yet the question as to the place of theology and the specific modes of thinking that it sponsors in Benjamin's variegated writings has long been contested.[3] On the one hand, there are those who regard Benjamin's perpetual work of conceptual unweaving and speculative demystification – to say nothing of his later, admittedly unorthodox, Marxian commitments – as radically incompatible with the gestures of theological investigation, so that the theological dimensions of his rhetorical figures are regarded as a mere residual attachment to an unacknowledged metaphysics, in short, an embarrassment about which progressively minded readers often prefer to remain silent. Such readers might subscribe to the notion that thematizing questions of religion and theology in his work only serves to perpetuate what Benjamin's contemporary Freud once called the future of an illusion. On the other hand, there are those readers for whom the relationship of Benjamin's texts to the signifying realm of theological discourse represent a welcome occasion to examine the relays between his work and the Bible, Jewish messianism, Zionism, his personal relationship to theological figures and thinkers of his time and the idea of theological inquiry as such. Significantly, Benjamin himself never accepted the notion of a binary opposition between the theologically saturated dimensions of his writings and his political commitments. As he emphasizes in a crucial letter to the Swiss writer and critic Max Rychner in 1931, 'if I were asked to express it in brief: I have never been able to conduct research and to write in anything other than, if I may put it this way, a theological sense [*theologischen Sinn*]—namely, in accordance with the Talmudic teaching about the forty-nine levels of meaning [*Sinnstufen*] in every passage of Torah'. Benjamin is quick to add: 'Well: In my experience, even the most pedestrian communist platitude possesses more *hierarchies of meaning* [*Hierachien des Sinnes*] than does today's bourgeois profundity [*Tiefsinn*], which always only has one meaning, that of an apologetic.'[4] Passages like this reinforce what has often been commented upon in Benjamin scholarship, namely, that, beginning in the late 1920s and early 1930s, Benjamin's mode of writing and thinking cannot be thought in separation from the particular constellation of theology and communism that came to inform the heterodox political dimension of his work ever more forcefully.[5] This idiosyncratic constellation left hardly anyone in Benjamin's inner circle satisfied: In Scholem's eyes, the mobilization of historical materialism only threatened to water down his friend's commitment to the central concerns of Jewish theology; Theodor W. Adorno bemoaned a lack of properly dialectical mediation; and Bertolt Brecht complains in his notebook of 1938 about his house guest in Danish exile: 'Benjamin is here … Everything is mysticism, in spite of all the anti-mysticist attitude. This is how the materialist view of history is being adapted! It is fairly horrific.'[6] But Benjamin's passage also suggests something more: If, for Benjamin, it is impossible to think and write outside of theological categories – which here, importantly, also means outside of categories requiring the conceptual labour of patient linguistic analysis, restless yet careful interpretation and caring textual exegesis – then the outcome of such interpretative labour cannot but have political implications that are not coextensive with an apology, even a tacit or unintended apology, of the status quo in a certain system of relations. Learning how to inherit Benjamin would entail learning how to confront this state of affairs.

Is it possible that the idea of a fully secularized, post-theological thinking emerges in Benjamin's writing as the sign of a premature foreclosure, a fallacy and a metaphysical aberration, even when his writing participates in the discourse of a radically secularizing dismantling of the category of the theological in all its political, cultural and aesthetic manifestations? In pursuing the implications of this question, our task is not to provide a panoramic overview of the theological motifs that permeate nearly all of Benjamin's most significant works, from the early esoteric writings and philosophy of language, via his Goethe essay and the *Trauerspiel* book, to his reflections on Kafka's Jewish motifs and the mechanical puppet at the beginning of his theses on the philosophy of history, as, for instance, the Protestant theologian Andreas Pangritz sets out to do in a circumspect manner.[7] We will not re-examine the possible relation between the late Benjamin's philosophy of history and the messianic tradition as it emerges in the Pauline Epistles, along the lines that Giorgio Agamben has begun to trace by means of the Pauline concept of a 'remaining time'.[8] No attempt will be made at providing a general account of the overall 'meaning' of theology for Benjamin's work in the way of critics such as Henning Günther; no extensive parallel reading of Benjamin will be conducted in relation to Scholem and Rosenzweig, as Stéphane Mosès has usefully begun; there will be no consideration of Benjamin's relation to Christian eschatology, as Josef Wohlmuth has offered; nor will there be an explicit discussion of specifically Jewish motifs in Benjamin's writings, as Irving Wohlfarth has provided.[9] Instead, my goal here is to confront the inheritance of Benjamin's uneasy legacy by providing critical commentary on a single passage from Convolute N, the epistemo-theoretical section of the *Passagen-Werk* – a work that deals obsessively with *passages* in the sense of the Parisian arcades but also in the sense of textual passages calling for ever-renewed interpretative attention – and to allow the singularity of this passage to provide a hint as to a more universal constellation of issues. I am guided here, among other things, by Pangritz's circumspect observation that, from the perspective of the field of theology, in the discussion of Benjamin 'theology is talked about in much too general terms [*viel zu pauschal von* Theologie *die Rede ist*]', even though I do not fully share – at least not without further consideration and qualification – the criticism implied in his view that 'Benjamin himself contributed to the confusion in that he, too, does not always make clear, which theology he means when he uses the word.'[10] After all, Benjamin's writing self-consciously refuses to provide stable concepts, for philosophical, literary and, not least of all, political reasons.[11] The case of theology, which functions as such a variegated and heterogeneous reservoir of discourse and reflection in his corpus, is no exception. I wish to suggest that the theological in Benjamin, whatever it will have turned out to be, can only ever be thought and talked about – that is, inherited – in relation to specific passages and contextual reinscriptions, which is to say, as matters of *language*, textual iterations that always point elsewhere to become what they are.

It may be one of the most fateful misunderstandings of reading and inheriting an intellectual legacy to believe, as a recent philosopher examining the dialectic of religico-eschatological transcendence in Benjamin does, 'that Benjamin's thought can be appropriated, in its core, independently of its often cryptic, literary form'.[12] From such a perspective, the rhetoricity of Benjamin's thinking becomes a mere afterthought to an a priori conceptual content that is considered to be thinkable exclusively as a product of reason, logic and full transparency, and which could theoretically have been expressed in this rhetorical form or that, *this* figure, metaphor, image *or another*. But what if Benjamin's conceptual concerns were fully inseparable from their specificity of form and their idiomatic linguistic staging, their particular *Sprachdenken*? The methodological gesture that I propose is largely a post-Hegelian one: to allow the particularity of the singular instance to manifest a universal concept without thereby becoming its mere illustration; and, dialectically, to allow the universal to travel through the singularity of the particular in order to become the object of a sensate cognition. Such a perspective requires textual singularity, because it cannot be talked about abstractly, that is, in isolation from the material inscriptions of Benjamin's language itself. In pursuing this path of reading and thinking, we also are guided once again by Benjamin's own professed method of 'erecting the great constructions from the smallest, sharply and cuttingly fitted building blocks' in a manner that asks us to 'recognize in the analysis of the small singular moment the crystal of the total event [*in der Analyse des kleinen Einzelmoments den Kristall des Totalgeschehens zu erkennen*].'[13] Yet it is important to recall that, for Benjamin, the glimpse of totality that may emerge in the analysis of the singular is always tied to its rhetorical specificity and in this way provides insight not into universality as such but rather into the universality of something particular, that is, the universality of singularity. In other words, the experience of learning from what is idiomatic and non-repeatable is itself a universal condition, and the model of learning that Benjamin proposes cannot be called a method in the sense that the Cartesian mathematically inclined tradition gives to the term. His perspective yields no system of stable, much less absolute, knowledge but is always a *textual* matter, a question of ceaseless interpretation in relation to specific texts and linguistically mediated problems, rather than general truth-claims about large concepts such as 'theology'. Let us therefore inherit the passage in question neither as theologians nor as philosophers, neither as historians nor as sociologists, but, more modestly, as readers.

To prepare for such an act of reading, we should note that Benjamin's passage will speak specifically of theology, rather than of religion, preferring a term of Ancient Greek origin over a Latin one. Theology is derived from the Greek *theologia*, itself comprised of *théos* (God) and *lógos* (study, sense, speech); it is the study of God or Gods and the scholarly engagement with the sources, scriptural or otherwise, undergirding belief. Religion, by contrast, derives from the Latin *religio*. According to Cicero, *religio* derives from *relegere*, meaning to regather, to reconsider, to reread; but according to Lactantius' later account, *religio* derives from *religare*, meaning to re-bind, and, by extension, to re-bind oneself, through faith, to the Divine.[14] (This latter sense of re-binding is also how Benjamin's friend Bloch derives the term religion). One may suggest that for Benjamin, although he uses the term theology, both the elements of a scholarly study of a divinity and its sources, and the question of careful rereading and rebinding that such study implies, are at issue.

As part of an attempted exposition of the general theoretical and speculative principles that inform his enigmatic work *Das Passagen-Werk* and, by extension, his mature writing as a whole, Benjamin offers the following enigmatic statement, which constitutes Convolute N 7a, 7:

> Mein Denken verhält sich zur Theologie wie das Löschblatt zur Tinte. Es ist ganz von ihr vollgesogen. Ginge es aber nach dem Löschblatt, so würde nichts, was geschrieben ist, übrig bleiben.[15]

In the now standard translation by Eiland and McLaughlin, the passage reads as follows:

> My thinking is related to theology as blotting paper is related to ink. It is saturated with it.
>
> Were one to go by the blotter, however, nothing of what is written would remain.[16]

In the earlier Hafrey and Sieburth translation, the passage is rendered thus:

> My thinking relates to theology the way a blotter does to ink. It is soaked through with it.
>
> If one were to go by the blotter, though, nothing of what has been written would remain.[17]

Both incisive translations of the three deceptively transparent-looking sentences are perfectly defensible. And yet, there are difficulties in rendering Benjamin's rhetorical figure of the *Löschblatt* that no English translation, however circumspect, can surmount.[18] This *linguistic* problem places us at the core of the *conceptual* difficulty of this passage, and it is worth lingering over. The semantic field of the closest terms that are available to us in English, 'blotting paper' and 'blotter', does not quite match the range of signification encompassed by *Löschblatt*. According to the *Oxford Dictionary and Thesaurus*, blotting paper refers to the 'unsized absorbent paper used for soaking up excess ink', as when school children practise writing the letters of the alphabet with a fountain pen (a custom still observed in the German school system today, which requires that a pupil 'graduate' from using a fountain pen before employing other writing utensils). A blotter is 'a sheet or sheets of blotting paper, usually inserted into a frame'.[19] But there is neither a frame in Benjamin's *Löschblatt*, nor the implication of a plurality of sheets, a dimension of meaning which would bestow on this image an empirical weight that would threaten to overwhelm its figurative singularity. What holds true in Freud's discussion of fetishism – that a fetishized object such as a shoe is imagined as singular in order to function as a fantasizable fetish, whereas picturing two shoes would merely return the fetishist to the shoes' utilitarian value of walking – holds true in Benjamin's rhetoric as well: For the image of the *Löschblatt* to work figuratively, it must be singular and not conjure the sense of multiple sheets, which would place us in an office supply store. Likewise, the term 'blotter' also refers, as Webster's dictionary reminds us, to 'a book in which entries (as of transactions or occurrences) are made temporarily pending their transfer to permanent record books', especially by the police.[20] This sense of a temporary inscription for later transfer, not to mention the legal associations that attach to this kind of blotter, is absent in *Löschblatt*. The German term, which literally means 'erasing paper', hinges on the word löschen, which can mean, among other things, to erase, to extinguish (a fire or a candle), to quench, to close, to delete, to strike out, to pay off (as in a debt), to clean, to wipe out, to remove, to switch off, to blot, but also to unload (in the sense of unloading the cargo of a ship). Among many other noun combinations formed with *löschen*, a *Feuerlöscher* is a fire extinguisher, a *Löschfahrzeug* is a fire engine, a *Löschkübel* is a fire bucket, the *Löschtaste* is the erase button, *Löschkalk* is slaked lime, and a *Löschzug* is a set of fire-fighting equipment.

In its etymology, *löschen* is related to the Anglo-Saxon *leskan* and *leskian*, and emerges out of the Middle High German *leschen* as well as the Old High German *lescan*. It constitutes a linguistic and conceptual extension of the word *liegen* (to lie, to lay) and in its original sense designated *sich legen* (to lie down). The most common combinations of *löschen* are found in such words as *erlöschen*, *verlöschen* and *auslöschen*; *löschen* as a strong verb has also merged with the transitive weak verb form of *löschen* that designates extinguishing and removal. The particular word formation *Löschblatt*, sometimes also rendered as *Löschpapier*, emerged in the German language in the seventeenth century.[21] According to the Grimms' *Deutsches Wörterbuch*, *Löschpapier*, which they define as '*papier zum ablöschen noch nasser schriftzüge* [paper for the erasing of still-wet traces of writing]', usually is a red or light grey color, and they cite, for illustrative purposes, the German dramatist August von Kotzebue's line '*warum so traurig? du siehst ja aus wie löschpapier!* [why so sad? you look like blotting paper!]' as well as the dramatist Gustav Freytag's reference to '*die reisekost, welche er in einem löschpapier umwickelt mitgenommen hatte* [the travel provisions which he had taken along wrapped in a piece of blotting paper]'.[22]

How, then, might we conceptualize Benjamin's thinking of *löschen* in his figure of the *Löschblatt*? Even Adorno, who in a May 1938 letter to Benjamin from Princeton alludes to this figure ('your simile of the *Löschblatt*') in passing, intuits the general importance of the image without interpreting it in any detail.[23] To begin with, we might note that what is at stake here is neither a static equivalence nor an economy of exchange but rather a question of *relation* ('verhält sich zu'). The quotidian application of a *Löschblatt* to the ink that it is meant to blot already produces a question of relation: the writing that is soaked up by the paper appears on it not as a straightforward copy but rather in inverted form, as if it were a kind of 'mirror writing' that must be read in a different way (allegorically, as it were, if we recall the original Greek meaning of *allegorein*, 'saying differently'), that is, both as itself and against the grain.[24] Allegorically, the *Löschblatt* holds up a mirror to writing itself, rendering it a self-reflexive terrain. Likewise, the application of the Löschblatt opens the question as to the relation between the two forms of ink with which it comes into contact on the page: Can it soak up excessive ink and stains without also soaking up the writing that is meant to remain? And how does the *Löschblatt* itself relate to the relation between word and smudge, writing and its surplus?

In fact, the specific constellation that Benjamin's image of the *Löschblatt* conjures is that of a double, even triple relation, since the *relation* of his thinking to theology itself *relates* to the *relation* of blotting paper and ink. This multiply coded *Verhältnis* in Benjamin's inquiry is concerned with specific ways of relating as such, that is, with ways of probing what *relating to* something means. From this particular perspective, the English phrase 'relates to', which perhaps comes closer to the non-static way in which Benjamin's German stages this relation – albeit without fully capturing the self-reflexivity emphasized by the pronoun 'sich' – may be preferable to its close relative, 'is related to', since the passive construction of that phrase may create the impression of a stable state of affairs that has been effected by an external agency, whereas the 'verhält *sich* zu' of Benjamin's original actively works to relate itself to something else. The self-reflexivity of the pronoun, in any event, introduces an element of unsettlingly active openness into the otherwise calm mode of a declarative sentence, implying a labour within the relation that is not unrelated to Hegel's emphasis on the labour of the concept, the precondition of all rigorous thought. It is this question of relating, and relating oneself to something, that informs so much of Benjamin's thinking, from his interpretation of the elective affinities among the chemical elements that structure the ways in which the characters of Goethe's novel relate to each other, all the way to the later question of how politics and its aestheticization relate in the mechanically repro-ducible work of art.

But the very question of relation deserves further attention. In his work *Of Minimal Things: Studies on the Notion of Relation*, Rodolphe Gasché provides a powerful reflection on the concept of relation as 'a limit-problem, an issue at the limit, to which all other questions of philosophy, large or small, are indebted and to which they must be traced back and related back'.[25] Conjuring the variegated conceptu-alizations of relation from Plato and Aristotle via Duns Scotus and Aquinas all the way to nineteenth- and twentieth-century philoso-phers such as Peirce, Frege, Russell, Whitehead, Nietzsche, Husserl, Heidegger and Derrida, along with writers such as Mallarmé, Kafka and Blanchot, he interrogates the ways in which, as 'minimal things, relations indeed refuse the identity of the concept', arguing that 'being-toward-another—*pros ti* or *esse ad*—is the essential peculi-arity of relation'.[26] According to this account, relation is the name par excellence for the question of what constitutes thinking itself and for how this thinking is fundamentally inflected by the position and movement of the other. There can be no identity without its essential relation to non-identity, no relation without the questioning of relationality itself. Here, 'being-toward-another presupposes a place of the other, a place that can be occupied by the opposite, or other, of the subject (entity or self) but which is not saturated, fulfilled, or exhausted by this occupation' so that, by extension, 'all relation involves a relation to the nonrelational that is something other than a negative modification of relationality'.[27] A rigorous thinking of relation would have to take into account the multiple modulations of relation itself, which may, among other things, take the form of 'encounter, arrival, address, contact, touch, belonging, distance, accord, agreement, determination, measuring, translation, and communication', and which may describe the movement of 'caesura, rhythm, and zigzag'.[28] The individual possible traits of a relation must themselves be related to their internal and external others, to the ways in which they make the thought of relationality both an imperative and an aporetic demand. How, then, can we think the relation that traverses Benjamin's thinking of the theological in a way that shows itself responsible to the multiplicity of the very idea of relationality and to the rigorous demands for reading and interpretation that this idea of the relation conjures? Is the posited relation one of touch or encounter? Or rather one of agreement, measuring or distance?

Benjamin's gesture (or is it a confession?), which thematizes the relation of his thinking to theology, allows for the distinct possibility of an attachment, albeit ever so fleeting, that others may be quick to dismiss. One thinks, for instance, of Nietzsche's radical statement in *The Anti-Christ* that his entire philosophy is the complete 'opposite' (*Gegensatz*) of the theological instinct and that 'what a theologian considers to be true *must* be false: in this, one almost has a criterion of truth'.[29] One also may think of the powerful language of Benjamin's contemporary, Martin Heidegger, who, after having turned from his theological roots to philosophy, asserts: 'Der Glaube hat im Denken keinen Platz [Belief has no place in thinking].'[30] This sentiment gains additional significance if we recall Heidegger's conceptualization of the discipline of philosophy as bound up in a metaphysics that is incapable of pursuing the rigorous and unsettling path of true thinking. It was in part because of this metaphysical predicament that the later Heidegger became concerned with the end of philosophy and the more essential task of *Denken* itself. But is this turn away from traditional philosophy toward *Denken*, too, the function of a belief – an article of faith that cannot be fully justified from within that which thinking can demonstrate? His best readers, including Jacques Derrida, have remarked on how difficult such statements are to accept, given his proto-Catholicism and the many figures and concepts – such as *Zusage*, *Mitsein* and *Bezeugung*, among others – that populate his writings and that, in their particular logic, cannot be dissociated fully from related questions of faith and belief.[31] If Heidegger generally prefers to postulate a non-relation between questions of belief and questions of thinking, Benjamin travels down the tracks of a different path – perhaps a mere *Holzweg*, as Heidegger would say, a wrong path or impasse – by inviting a thinking of the relational character of his thinking as a significant dimension of thinking itself, especially a thinking of the relation between thinking and relation.

From another perspective, the relation that Benjamin wishes to think is at least in some respects closer to the logic followed by his personal friend and formative early influence, Bloch. The young Benjamin received decisive impulses from the theologico-political argumentations of Bloch's early *Spirit of Utopia*. Although he could be almost as critical of Bloch's modes of inquiry as was Adorno when the latter once derisively referred to Bloch as 'ein Buber ohne Bart [a

Buber without a beard]', Benjamin's way of relating to theological and
epistemo-political paradoxes is not unrelated to some of Bloch's best
moments. In one of his least-read but strongest works, *Atheism in
Christianity*, Bloch, from a Marxian perspective, suggestively argues
that the 'best thing about religion is that it produces heretics' and 'only
an atheist can be a good Christian; only a Christian can be a good
atheist' in a posture that seeks 'to transcend without transcendence'.[32]
The relationality between faith and reason, belief and epistemologi-
cally mediated liberation, the inside and the outside of a discursive
formation of transcendence is here called into question, allowing for
a renewed thinking of belief and its supposed other.

What, then, are we to make of the triple relation that Benjamin
himself wishes to think here ('Mein Denken verhält sich zur
Theologie')? It is *his* thinking ('Mein Denken') that, significantly,
compels him to begin his sentence with the pronoun of the first-
person singular mode. *His* thinking is at stake, rather than someone
else's, affirming through the first-person singular not simply a mode
of subjectivity but rather a particular situatedness out of which this
thinking emerges – even if 'my' thinking ultimately also must be
'your' thinking if it is to be verifiable by shared laws such as the
non-self-contradictory requirements of logic and the methodical
repeatability and relative justifiability of this or that truth claim.
'My' thinking, Benjamin writes, relates, relates itself to ('verhält sich
zu') – and it *is*, in fact, that which relates, which is to say, embodies
another name for relation. There is no thinking without relation,
without a *Verhältnis* and without a *verhalten zu*.[33] If the logic of
Benjamin's relational simile lines up thinking with the *Löschblatt* and
theology with ink, then the activity of producing language, gener-
ating text, is on the side of ink, that is, of theology. Theology is that
which generates writing, belief and presentation, while thinking,
perhaps not unlike the so-called destructive character who plays
such a crucial role in Benjamin's essay of the same name, is there to

cancel, to erase, to undo, to extinguish – perhaps even to unload. If theology is concerned with belief, then thinking is concerned with questioning, reason, logic and argumentative rigor. Like the two hands of Derrida's Hegelian commentary in *Glas*, one writing and the other erasing, the ink of theology produces text that thinking works to wipe out. Are we in the realm delimited by the juxtaposition of faith and reason, *Glaube* and *Vernunft*, to use the terms of the theological conversation between Jürgen Habermas and Cardinal Ratzinger, later Pope Benedikt XVI?[34]

'Mein Denken verhält sich zur Theologie,' Benjamin writes, 'wie das Löschblatt zur Tinte': thinking is that which appears to threaten, through its erasures, what theology gives us to believe. In fact, the figure of the *Löschblatt* here is said to be 'ganz von ihr [der Theologie] vollgesogen', fully saturated with theology, or, as Hafrey and Sieburth hear it, 'soaked through with it'. And yet, there is a limit to how much a *Löschblatt* can soak up; its holding and cleaning power is finite. Has this point of being fully saturated ('ganz vollgesogen') been reached in spite of the *Löschblatt*'s attempt to soak up even more, that is, in spite of thinking's attempts at erasing the theological – or has the blotting paper of thought voluntarily ceased its activity in light of the fact that, if it continued, nothing that was written would remain at all ('nichts, was geschrieben ist, übrig bleibt')? In other words, does Benjamin wish us to conceptualize the failure of the *Löschblatt* or its success? To what extent can we think of the *Löschblatt* as a successful failure, a mode of failing successfully? After all, the movement of the *Löschblatt* works to erase all that has been believed and written. Neither of the published translations, in which 'Ginge es aber nach dem Löschblatt' is rendered, respectively, as 'Were one to go by the blotter' and 'If one were to go by the blotter', while perfectly reasonable, can quite capture the quasi-voluntary dimension that Benjamin inscribes in the figure of the *Löschblatt*, almost as though it had a will of its own. 'Ginge es aber nach dem Löschblatt' means 'But if the blotting paper had its way'. Unlike the phrase 'if one were to go by the blotter', which suggests that the *Löschblatt* could be considered by someone external to it as one standard of measurement among others, in the original version the *Löschblatt* has indicated a preference, has made a plea, that is, the plea to be allowed to erase everything by soaking it all up, and that plea is now on the table as a request either to be granted or denied. These linguistic subtleties in the translation of the German reflexive form matter because the passage in which they are embedded is concerned, precisely, with the question of relation and of agency – who does what to whom – so that the textual cannot be thought in separation from the conceptual, or rhetoric apart from logic.

But is the request by the *Löschblatt* granted? Benjamin does not provide a direct answer, yet the mood of the verb 'gehen', which is here rendered in its subjunctive form 'ginge', evokes a hypothetical situation through a subtle shift between the German letters 'e' and 'i' that implies that its wish has become a matter of debate, the subject of a 'what if' scenario that has not yet been decided. After all, the sentence does not preclude the possibility that the decision to erase fully may, in fact, reside with the *Löschblatt* – especially if we take seriously the interpretation of the *Löschblatt* as a figure of Benjamin's thinking as such, which, ultimately, has jurisdiction over its own conceptual and textual production. It is therefore not enough to say that the hypothetical statement here is simply counterfactual, as it would have been in the subjunctive past perfect. That is, if Benjamin had written 'wäre es aber nach dem Löschblatt gegangen [had the blotting paper had its way]', the implication would have been that it in fact did not and that Benjamin's thinking, along with the blotting paper, had, in fact, taken a different turn. Rather, by self-consciously mobilizing the present tense subjunctive mood, Benjamin's last sentence keeps the outcome suspended, thereby maintaining the problem around which it circles as an open question and as a matter of debate.

Does thinking wish to do what the *Löschblatt* wishes to do – to erase fully? Or is it at odds with the *Löschblatt*'s wishes, in which case the passage should be interpreted as introducing a split between thinking and the very figure that it itself had set out to employ as a stand-in for that thinking? Does Benjamin's thinking wish to erase theology or (also) keep it alive? We should recall that the function of the *Löschblatt* itself is not as unequivocal as it may at first appear. To be sure, a *Lösch-blatt* is literally an erasing paper, yet what it typically erases is not the entire ink on a sheet but rather only the excess, in an attempt to prevent the desired writing on a page from becoming illegible, either through accidental smudging or through unintended contact with the excess ink surrounding it. That is to say, while the *Löschblatt* can be thought of as that which erases, it also, by erasing in a strategic way, preserves the text. In fact, its most common, intended use is that it erases *in order to* preserve. Likewise, the ink that is soaked up by the *Löschblatt* does not disappear for good but rather survives in the *Löschblatt* itself, until the entire *Löschblatt* has turned the colour of the ink it has soaked up. It is helpful here to recall Hegel's concept of the *Aufhebung*, usually translated by the English neologism 'sublation'. The noun *die Aufhebung* and the verb from which it stems, *aufheben*, in German possess the contra-dictory meanings of cancellation and preservation (in addition to the empirical meaning of picking or lifting something up with one's hand, *etwas mit der Hand aufheben*). Consider the three meanings of *aufheben* in our context: Picking up the *Löschblatt* with one's hand, one both cancels and preserves, erasing the ink and allowing it to survive in a sublated form elsewhere. This restless dialectic of the *Aufhebung* of the *Löschblatt* cannot be reduced to the stability of a concept that would be capable of describing once and for all how blotting paper and ink, thinking and theology, relate to each other.

The heterodox figure of the *Löschblatt* that Benjamin mobilizes can be said, at least in part, to be inherited from, and inflected by, a

mystical tradition traversing certain gestures of Judaism. According
to Scholem's explication of the religious categories of revelation and
tradition in Judaism, the Torah – the religious doctrine embodied in
the first five books of the Bible – is to be imagined as a book containing
only blank pages, so that the original written form of the Torah can be
conceptualized as an interpretation or belated commentary upon the
invisible *ur*-text. As Scholem suggests, it is not 'the blackness of the
writing traced out by the ink' that is to be understood as 'the actual
written Torah', but rather 'the mystical whiteness of the letters on
the roll of parchment on which nothing can be seen'.[35] It is as though
the workings of Benjamin's theological figure of the *Löschblatt* were
indirectly evoked, in part, both by this original conception of the Torah
as the mysteriously unreadable text and by Kafka's implicit reference
to this image of the Torah in his novel fragment *The Castle* (written in
1922 and published in 1926), in which the protagonist K. at one point
observes: "'You are interpreting ... the letter so well that finally nothing
remains other than the signature on a blank sheet of paper.'"[36] Here, the
meaning of religious doctrine is not an a priori stable category waiting
to be hermeneutically consumed. Rather, it is only through what we
might call the countersignature of the critic, that is, through the patient
reading, interpreting and therefore rewriting of the text, that the logic
and sense of what is written is imagined to reveal itself. In this patient
deferral of stable meaning through the critical and interpretative act,
the invisible words on the blank pages fluctuate between being made
visible (through the addition of other words) and being erased as
lexemes enabling the transmission of a meaning. Black and white, ink
and blank paper, inscription and its erasure, visibility and its absence,
legibility and its unavailability enter a serious dance of binarisms in
which the signifying power of language itself is at stake – and, through
it, the intelligibility of theological modes of thinking as such.

From the dual perspective of the question concerning the invisible
text and the question concerning the problem of relation that the

Löschblatt brings into exacting relief, Benjamin cannot quite be said to share the pragmatico-ideological terms suggested by the analysis of his interlocutor Brecht. Brecht, in his short text 'Die Frage, ob es einen Gott gibt' (The question of whether there is a God), collected in his so-called *Herr Keuner* stories, writes: 'Someone asked Herr K. if there is a God. Herr K. said: "My advice to you is to think about whether your behavior would change depending on the answer to this question. If nothing would change, then we can drop the question. If it would change, then I can at least help you by telling you that you already have decided: You need a God."'[37] For Brecht's Keuner figure, the question concerning a God can only be cast in terms of its use value, that is, not ontologically – or even theologically – but only functionally within a system of relations. For Benjamin, the question is differently accentuated. For him, the question is neither merely one of decision nor of exposing the latent and unacknowledged need for a transcendental signified that in turn is to be seen primarily in terms of its functionality within the discourse of an ideological self-negotiation. Rather, Benjamin trains his critical vigilance on the scandal of the latent presence of theological remnants – and even revenants – in a gesture of critique that believes itself to have overcome its filiation with any *théos* through avowedly anti-theological gestures of separation and erasure.

It is the *Löschblatt*'s multiply coded sublation that embodies such a scandal in Benjamin's thinking. It is a scandal that even a dialectical thinker such as Max Horkheimer is hesitant to accept. In a letter to Benjamin dated 16 March 1937 – partially cited by Benjamin in Convolute N 8, 1, that is, in very close proximity to the preceding blotting paper entry – Horkheimer queries one of the philosophical motifs that had occupied Benjamin at least since the earliest formulations of the *Trauerspiel* material: the non-closure (*Unabgeschlossenheit*) of history: 'The determination of the non-closure is idealistic if closure is not included in it.' Horkheimer continues: 'Past injustice

has occurred and is a matter of closure. The slain are really slain
… If one takes non-closure entirely seriously, one must believe in
the Last Judgment … This holds first and foremost for individual
being-in-the-world [*Dasein*], in which it is not the happiness but
the unhappiness that is sealed by death.' Horkheimer's worry is
that Benjamin's conception refuses to acknowledge the concrete
and actual distress that accompanies injustice and the infliction of
needless human suffering. From this perspective, the belief in, or
philosophical diagnosis of, non-closure would appear, at best, as the
expression of an overly optimistic hope for a transcendental reversal
of the meaning of suffering, and, at worst, as a denial of the finality
of some acts, experiences or instances of (fatal) injustice. Benjamin
reflects on Horkheimer's objections – and his suspicions of Benjamin's
latent theological idealism – by suggesting that 'history is not exclusively a science [*Wissenschaft*] but also and not least a form of
remembrance or mindfulness [*Eingedenken*] … . Such remembrance
or mindfulness can make the non-closed (happiness) into something
closed, and the closed (suffering) into something non-closed.' He
goes on to concede that 'this is theology; but in remembrance or
mindfulness we have an experience that forbids us to grasp history
as fundamentally atheological, little as it is allowable for us to
attempt to write it with immediately theological concepts [*so wenig
wir sie in unmittelbar theologischen Begriffen zu schreiben versuchen
dürfen*].'[38] The unusual word *Eingedenken*, which Benjamin also
uses in such other areas of his corpus as his reflections on Proustian
mémoire involontaire and on the discourse of autobiography in
Berlin Chronicle, is itself borrowed from the tradition of German
mysticism and is not normally found in German dictionaries. It
imbricates the verb *gedenken* (to remember in a ceremonial way) and
the predicate adjective *eingedenk* (to be mindful of, to be aware of),
suggesting the intellectually mediated confluence of a calmly attuned
remembrance and an especially alert mindfulness.[39] We might say

that one of the key modes of remembrance, for Benjamin, resides in the phenomenon of mindfulness in relation to the idea that the attainment of historical and philosophical insight, at least in the orbit of his writing, cannot be separated from a perpetual obsessive reflection on that insight's imbrication in theological modes as well as in a resistance to the false immediacy that they often propagate. His thinking works with and against the theological, following it only by breaking with it, and, by breaking with it, also following it – as though it were a theology without theology, an atheological theology at odds with itself. Benjamin's sentences about the *Löschblatt* are, like all his sentences, not instantiations of a classically conceived negative theology but rather inscriptions of a perpetually vigilant and reflective writing and erasing.

With respect to the work performed by the atheologically theological *Löschblatt*, 'nothing would remain [*würde nichts übrig bleiben*]', Benjamin writes. Nothing that was written would survive, as if it were the allusive antipode of another phrase of which Benjamin always was fond: to read what was never written. And yet, the ink marks comprising the famously microscopic sentences produced by his fountain pen remain; indeed, they have given us the 14 volumes of his oeuvre to read. Likewise, theology remains a spectral presence in his thinking not only as a sublated material substance but also as an open question – more precisely, as an abiding question of relation. Have we begun to understand the implications of the figure of the *Löschblatt* and of the subjunctive mood that Benjamin gives us to ponder without providing the sense of resolution that would attend a decisive gesture of affirmation or negation? In inheriting Benjamin, we cannot know – only think, only believe, without these two modes of experience ever becoming fully congruent.

The view that Benjamin's dialectical image of the *Löschblatt* opens up for us is one in which the negative dialectic of thinking and theology, of demystification and an alleged transcendental signified, of preservation and erasure, of fixing and smudging, refuses to be arbitrarily and prematurely terminated. Instead, it requires an unyielding vigilance of thinking, a thinking that also must take account of the very conditions that first make thinking possible. The philosophical, ethical and political necessity of a ceaseless and rigorous reflection on the constellation of thinking, writing and believing is one of the lessons to be learned from Benjamin's inheritance, if there are any. From Benjamin's perspective, to assume that our *Löschblatt* has done its job well, perhaps all too well – in other words, to believe that our thinking has finally overcome theology for good, that it is no longer tacitly attached to a residual, unsublatable and unacknowledged theological commitment – may well turn out to be the *most theological position of all*.

Let us therefore break off by posing two Gretchen-questions:

Do we *know* this or do we *believe* it?
And can we *relate*?

Critique and the Thing:
Benjamin and Heidegger

In memoriam
Marc Eli Blanchard (1942–2009)
scholar and resistance fighter
in the belly of the beast

I.

The modern concept of critique that Kant mobilizes in the *Critique of Pure Reason* became decisive for all philosophical engagements with critique that followed it, that is, inherited it. In his Preface to the 1781 edition, Kant argues that 'our age is the genuine age of *critique*, to which everything must submit'. He then goes on to explain the role that critique ought to play from that point forward. Critique is to respond to the demand 'that reason should take on anew the most difficult of all its tasks, namely, that of self-knowledge, and institute a court of justice [*einen Gerichtshof einzusetzen*], by which reason may secure its rightful claims while dismissing its groundless pretensions … and this court is none other than the *critique of pure reason* itself'. Kant elaborates: 'Yet by this I do not understand a critique of books and systems, but a critique of the faculty of reason in general, in respect of all the cognitions after which reason might strive *independently of all experience*, and hence the decision about the possibility or impossibility of a metaphysics in general.'[1] If the task of critique as a form of knowledge and self-knowledge is to function as a court of law, a *Gerichtshof* for thought itself, then critique is charged not merely with criticizing existing structures and practices from a perspective external to them but also, first and foremost, with formalizing the general laws and principles that establish the conditions and frameworks whereby possibilities of meaning are created by consciousness prior to its encounter with an object of sense perception. In other words, the form of critique envisioned by Kant inquires into the fundamental conditions of possibility for judgement and experience. But Kant's *Gerichtshof*, as a court of law constituted by the rigors of critique itself rather than by the require-ments of some external agency, must constantly work to establish the protocols of reading and interpreting according to which it could pass judgement (*richten*). In order to get it right (*richtig*), those who preside over this court as critics or judges (*Richter*) are called upon perpetually to question the assumptions and procedures that orient (*ausrichten*) their thinking in light of the need for a critique that is the self-critique of reason. We might say, therefore, that the legacy of post-Kantian critique unfolds under the sign of a triple demand: to advance a critical perspective on the object; to delimit the parameters that establish critique as a self-critique of the principles of reason; and to conceive of critique as a self-constitutive praxis that takes itself as its object in a self-reflexive examination of its own presuppositions and processes.

Central among those in the twentieth century who inherited the variegated legacy of the Kantian *Gerichtshof* of critique were Walter Benjamin and Martin Heidegger, thinkers who, while contemporary to each other (Benjamin was three years younger than Heidegger), are seldom read together in a sustained manner.[2] And perhaps, it could be argued, it is better that way. For what would it mean to 'compare' two philosophers whose idiomatic and unmistakably singular signatures sponsor radically different perspectives and truth claims? Will anything ever be gained, one might ask, by comparing a great philosophical work, literary text, painting or piece of music to something else? After all, comparison is vulnerable to arbitrariness, exhaustion and boredom, because anything can always be compared with anything else. Even the habitual, and perhaps too thoughtless, statement, 'You cannot compare the two', is implicitly based on a prior (and likely unspoken) comparison that has led the speaker to the conclusion that two things cannot be compared; but even here, the demand for non-comparison is based on a prior comparison. Is, therefore, that which is most valuable not lodged precisely in the endeavour to compare something not with something else but *with itself*? This mode of self-comparison requires a form of radically engaged reading and interpreting, a commitment actually to enter the inner world and logic of this particular artwork or this particular text and to do justice to what is most distinctive and idiosyncratic about it.

But it is also in comparison to something else that what is most specific about a work or a thought is cast into rigorous relief. Only by understanding how *this* work differs from *that* work, regardless of the modes of self-differentiation that may be operative within the individual works, can the singularity of something fully emerge. There is, hence, a form of comparison that *singularizes*. Yet even this singularization, meant to make specificity visible, can, through excessive comparison, also make specificity disappear. As the philosopher Berel Lang once aptly put it in relation to Heidegger's later silence with respect to his political commitments during the Third Reich, 'one way to make something disappear is to place it, like a grain of sand in the desert, in a mass of supposed likeness'.[3] While one's initial impetus for comparing a grain of sand with other grains may well have been to bring to the fore precisely that which makes the initial grain of sand singular and specific, in fact different from all other grains of sand, there comes a point – and it is not at all certain that this point is merely a numerical one – when the act of comparison begins to move from the specification of difference to its eradication.

And yet, as Friedrich Hölderlin, the poet to whose textual legacy both Benjamin and Heidegger dedicated some of their most important texts, knew, 'it is lovely to compare'. When we set out to compare two writers as idiosyncratic and as influential as Benjamin and Heidegger, a few basic facts should be borne in mind. Benjamin, an anti-fascist, dialectically oriented, academically marginalized German-Jewish writer who committed suicide while attempting to escape Nazi persecution, was often highly sceptical of Heidegger's ontological project, writing to Gershom Scholem on 20 January 1930 that 'I will find Heidegger on my path, and I expect sparks will fly from the shock of the confrontation.'[4] And Heidegger, a securely installed university professor, and later rector, with sympathies during the 1930s for the National Socialist movement, provides no evidence of ever having seriously engaged, or even read, a single text by Benjamin. We do know, however, that after World War II when Benjamin's and Heidegger's mutual close friend Hannah Arendt – a former student of Heidegger's whose first husband was also Benjamin's cousin – returned to Freiburg to present a lecture on Benjamin on 26 July 1967, Heidegger, whose infamous meeting with the poet Paul Celan had occurred in his Todtnauberg hut the day before, was present in the audience, and he discussed Arendt's Benjamin lecture with her the following day.[5] In the extended published version of her text on Benjamin, Arendt states: 'Without realizing it, Benjamin actually had more in common with Heidegger's remarkable sense for living eyes and living bones that had sea-changed into pearls and coral, and as such could be saved and lifted into the present only by doing violence to their context in interpreting them with "the deadly impact" of new thoughts, than he did with the dialectical subtleties of his Marxist friends.'[6] And recently it has been suggested, based on evidence found in a little-known text by Heidegger on Raphael's Sistine Madonna that was first published in 1955 under the title 'Über die Sixtina', that he had read Benjamin's 'The Work of Art in the Age of Its Technical

Reproducibility', whose third version includes an extensive footnote to Hubert Grimme's work on Raphael's Madonna, a work Benjamin also had emphasized in his earlier review essay 'The Rigorous Study of Art'.[7]

On the systematic level of their respective ways of thinking and writing, we might say that, for all that separates them, Benjamin and Heidegger also are connected in important and often unacknowledged ways that directly concern the content and implications of some of their core concepts. These include their shared interest in the complex relationship between construction and destruction (Benjamin's *Destruktion* and Heidegger's *Abbau*); the fate of the work of art and the aesthetic under conditions of modernity (Benjamin's *Reproduzierbarkeit* and Heidegger's *Ur-sprung*); the question of technology in relation to consciousness and thinking (Benjamin's *Zerstreuung* and Heidegger's *Gestell*); the poetry of Hölderlin; the question of what constitutes an image (Benjamin's *dialektisches Bild* and Heidegger's *eidos*); the theory and practice of translation (Benjamin's *Übersetzbarkeit* and Heidegger's *Über-setzen*); the significance of thinking forms of historicity (Benjamin's *Jetzt-Zeit* and Heidegger's *Geschichtlichkeit*) rather than conventional history; their perpetual return to and transformation of Kant; and, perhaps above all, their common effort to approach phenomena rigorously through a textually and linguistically mediated model. One might call this model a *Sprachdenken*, a sustained, caring and careful approach that emphasizes the role played by *language* in the formation of thought and culture. This shared emphasis regards language not primarily as an instrument of communication or as the cognitive attestation of an extra-linguistic reality that waits to be referenced by a speaker but rather as an elusively self-referential condition of possibility in living, thinking and acting that never can be reduced to the recording, transmission and reception of a stable meaning.[8] The image of Benjamin and Heidegger as absolute opposites, even antipodes, legitimate as it often may be, should not, as the British critic Howard Caygill once elegantly put it, become 'a sentimental idyll, a "left melancholic" alibi for not examining the possible complicity between their ... views', which only would serve to 'sacrifice the light ... cast upon prevailing assumptions about the relationship between history, politics, and art under modernity'.[9]

Bearing this context in mind, I wish to suggest that in spite of the many undeniable, and often unbridgeable, differences between the two with respect to philosophical, political, historical and personal matters, Benjamin and Heidegger share a fundamental set of concerns. They inherit along similar lines of flight. Both thinkers' projects can be read as sustained engagements with the Kantian inheritance of critique in a way that deviates markedly from the neo-Kantianisms that were prevalent in German-speaking countries during Benjamin's and Heidegger's years of intellectual formation. In their inheritance of Kant, both Benjamin and Heidegger recognize that critique derives from the Greek *krinein,* which means to separate, to choose and to decide, but also is the climax or turning point in the course of an illness. The two writers, albeit from differing perspectives, each mobilize the concept of *Kritik* in relation to Kant's canonical account of critique as transcendental philosophy in the terms initially outlined in the First Critique. While Benjamin seeks to stage critique as a mode of thought distinct from the operations of commentary (for instance, in his seminal essay on 'Goethe's Elective Affinities'), Heidegger relates his reading of Kant's concept to the question of what constitutes a 'thing', *ein Ding.* Of particular interest are the ways in which each thinker surprisingly establishes a relationship between critique and the question of the thing or 'thingness' – as a cultural object and also as formal mode of intellectual intuition – giving rise to new and deeper understandings of the striking similarities and differences between textually mediated forms of dialectical materialism and fundamental ontology. While Benjamin works to inherit Kantian *Kritik* dialectically in order to fashion himself as belonging to the critics whom he characterizes as *Physiognomen der Dingwelt* or physiognomists of the world of things, Heidegger inherits the Kantian problematic of *Kritik* in terms of an unexpected and far-reaching positivity, especially in such works as 'Das Ding' and in his lecture course on Kant, entitled *Die Frage nach dem Ding*. It is perhaps no accident at all, then, that Arendt in her conjunction of Benjamin and Heidegger mobilizes the trope of *things* – eyes, bones, pearls, coral – to concretize the thinkers' strange common orbit. But this shared orbit is determined not primarily by concerns of classic phenomenology, the call by Heidegger's teacher Edmund Husserl to return 'to the things themselves' and to read the phenomena of one's *Lebenswelt* accordingly, but rather by a commitment to a creative inheritance, that is, to rethinking, in relation to the thing, a possible practice of critique in a transformative post-Kantian vein.

II.

Let us backtrack, turning first to Benjamin's inheritance. It is well known that a perpetual confrontation with the concept and the praxis of *Kritik* occupies a central role throughout his entire corpus. For instance, the young Benjamin of 'The Life of Students' (1915) already understood the 'sole task of critique' as being to 'liberate what is to come from its deformation in the present by an act of cognition'.[10] Subsequent to that Benjamin wished to become the 'most significant critic' of German literature, and, later, in 1931, he began to compose a text to be entitled 'Die Aufgabe des Kritikers' ('The Task of the Critic') – an essay that was to give a general theoretical account on the model of his earlier 'Die Aufgabe des Übersetzers' ('The Task of the Translator'), but which survives today only in the form of notes.[11] Later still, Benjamin made plans

with his friend Bertolt Brecht jointly to establish a new journal
entitled *Krise und Kritik*, a project that never came to fruition. What
is perhaps less well appreciated, however, is the extent to which the
Kantian concept of critique inflected Benjamin's understanding
of his own engagement with critique. As early as 1917, Benjamin
writes to Scholem that 'no matter how great the number of Kantian
minutiae that may have to fade away', he is capable of envisioning
his own critical project only 'by means of the revision and further
development of Kant' and 'the only thing I see clearly is the task
… that what is *essential* in Kant's thought must be preserved'.[12] The
first sustained Benjaminian text to emerge from this simultaneous
appropriation and development of Kantian critique is 'Program
for a Coming Philosophy' (1917–18) and its articulation of the
critical possibility of creating a form of Kantian critique oriented
toward a thinking yet to come. But it is not until Benjamin's essay
on Goethe's *Elective Affinities*, begun shortly after his Kant essay
and eventually published in 1924–5, that Benjamin finds a critical
mode that he considers, as he indicates in a letter to Scholem,
both a piece of 'exemplary critique [*exemplarische Kritik*]' and a
decisive 'prolegomenon to certain purely philosophical exposi-
tions [*Vorarbeit zu gewissen rein philosophischen Darlegungen*]'.[13]
The exemplarity of Benjamin's Goethe essay could be said to be
operative on at least three levels: it constitutes a prime example of
Benjamin's mode of self-reflexive critique; it takes as its object one
of the exemplary novels of *the* exemplary classical German writer;
and it indirectly unfolds in the orbit of Friedrich Schlegel's critique
of another novel by Goethe, *Wilhelm Meister's Apprenticeship*, a
piece of critique taken to be exemplary of Early German Romantic
literary theory.[14]

What, for Benjamin, distinguishes critique from the related form of
commentary is, among other things, the fact that it always is oriented
towards the truth content of the artwork: 'Critique seeks the truth

content [*Wahrheitsgehalt*] of a work of art; commentary, its material content [*Sachgehalt*]. The relation between the two is determined by that basic law of literature according to which the more significant the work, the more inconspicuously and intimately its truth content is bound up with its material content.'[15] In this sense, critique, as the praxis of *krinein*, draws on the shifting and inconstant figures of separation that characterize truth content and material content. 'If,' Benjamin writes, 'to use a simile, one views the growing work as a burning funeral pyre, then the commentator stands before it like a chemist, the critic like an alchemist. Whereas, for the former, wood and ash remain the sole objects of his analysis, for the latter only the flame itself preserves an enigma: that of what is alive. Thus, the critic inquires into the truth, whose living flame continues to burn over the heavy logs of what is past and the light ashes of what has been experienced.'[16] According to this image, critique has its source in a flickering, dangerous flame in whose light what is to be separated is both seen for the first time and burned to ash. These cinders and ashen traces continue to testify to what was separated by critique, even if what has been separated in this way only can be thought as absence, or as a presence that has fled into a vast, unapproachable distance.

The concept of critique that Benjamin wishes to think toward is indebted both to the fundamental Kantian articulation and to the Early Romantic development of the concept, especially that of Friedrich Schlegel. Schlegel's theory of critique made a more profound impression on Benjamin than other historical attempts at furthering and reorienting Kant's concept of critique, including even Fichte's concept of critique as abstract negation and Herder's attempted system of a so-called meta-critique.[17] In his programmatic 1804 essay 'On the Essence of Critique', Schlegel gives shape to the German Romantics' notion of critique as the progressive mediator between philosophy and history. He writes:

We should think of critique as a middle term between history and philosophy, one that shall join them both, and in which both are to be united to form a new, third term. Without philosophical spirit, such a critique cannot thrive—everyone agrees on this—nor without historical knowledge. The philosophical elaboration and examination of history and of traditions is unquestionably critique. But any historical view of philosophy is, just as unquestionably, critique as well. It is apparent that the compilation of opinions and systems that is usually called philosophy cannot be meant here … . We may bring together the most solid results of a historical mass under a concept, or else we may specify a concept not merely in order to allow distinctions, but rather to construct the concept in its becoming, from its earliest origins to its final completion, giving this, together with the concept, its own inner history. Both of these are characterization, the highest task of critique and the most intimate union of history and philosophy.[18]

If it is true, as one reader aptly puts it, that the general orientation of Benjamin's project is to invent a 'thinking which attempts to utter in critique the truth that denies itself to any philosophical system',[19] then Schlegel's definition of critique as the mediator between philosophy and history provides us with a clue as to Benjamin's path. Conventional forms of philosophy and historiography are not sufficient to perform their own work while also taking into account the important insights generated by the other. It is in critique that the dialogue between them takes place. At the same time, critique is neither a system nor a method, neither a task to be fulfilled nor a predetermined intervention to be executed upon the world of things. Rather, critique is a perpetual engagement with itself, not in the sense of an endlessly narcissistic self-reflection but rather in the sense of a self-conscious commitment to reinvestigating, even reinventing, on the most rigorous level imaginable, its assumptions and procedures with each new object.

It is no accident, therefore, that critique – pushed to the extreme position of a perpetual self-definition – comes to play a significant role in Benjamin's 1920 doctoral dissertation on the theory of art criticism in German Romanticism. There, in the course of providing a brief genealogy of the modern term 'critique', Benjamin writes that, of 'all the technical terms of philosophy and aesthetics in the works of the early Romantics, the words "critique" and "critical" are easily the most often encountered'. He continues: 'Through Kant's philosophical work, the concept of critique had acquired for the younger generation an almost magical meaning'. For Romantics such as Novalis and Schlegel as well as 'for speculative philosophy, the term "critical" meant objectively productive, creative out of thoughtful deliberation. To be critical meant to elevate thinking so far beyond all restrictive conditions that the knowledge of truth sprang forth … from insight into the falsehood of these restrictions'.[20] If to practise critique means to push thinking beyond its presumed limits and to submit to scrutiny the very idea of a delimited thinking, the critical stance that Benjamin envisions starts with the restlessness of a negativity rather than with the assured imposition of external critical standards onto an object or idea. To practise critique in this way is to remain open to its difficulties, its others, even the perpetual threat of its impossibility, an uncontainable threat which makes it a form of critical potentiality in the first place.

While Benjamin's concept of critique and its practice is heavily inflected by that of both Kant and the Romantics, what distinguishes it, among other things, is the insistence on articulating the relationship not only between philosophy and history, critique and reason or critique and forms of consciousness, but also between critique and the thing (*das Ding*). It is not a coincidence that in the *Arcades Project* he evokes the image of collectors and, by extension, himself as an obsessive collector of things, as 'physiognomists of the world of things [*Physiognomen der Dingwelt*]'.[21] To practise the kind of philosophical, literary, aesthetic and cultural critique that Benjamin has in mind, the critic must learn how to read *die Dinge*, the things that, at times inexplicably, inhabit his world. As one of Benjamin's German editors, Rolf Tiedemann, reminds us in his introduction to the first publication of the *Arcades Project* in 1982, the 'prolegomena to a materialist physiognomics that can be gleaned from the *Passagen-Werk* counts among Benjamin's most prodigious conceptions'.[22] Learning to practise critique by way of a consideration of, and perpetual re-engagement with, the thing-world means learning to read the thing as though it were a text, to be read and reinterpreted again and again, until 'the real can be read like a text [*das Wirkliche wie einen Text lesen*]'.[23]

It is this thing-orientation of critique that Benjamin's essay on Goethe's novel makes vivid. There, we are told that 'because what is eternal in the work stands out only against the ground of those realities, every contemporary critique, however eminent, comprehends in the work more the moving truth than the resting truth, more the temporal effect than the eternal being'. Benjamin continues by suggesting that 'the most essential contents of being-in-the-world [*wesentlichsten Inhalte des Daseins*] are capable of stamping their imprint on the world of things [*Dingwelt*], indeed that without such imprinting they are incapable of fulfilling themselves'.[24] To interrogate modes of being in the world, critique in the Benjaminian sense fastens upon those things that not only represent what they themselves are – this chair, this desk, this toy – but also bear the inscription of existence that the *Dingwelt* to which they belong has bestowed upon them. The thing is that which presents the material manifestation of existence to itself as a system of signs to be interpreted by the physiognomist of the world of things.

We have known for a while that Benjamin's own obsession with the *Dingwelt* compelled him to collect myriad things, including children's books and snow globes, and to comment on the appearance, for instance, of small marzipan figurines. Likewise, we have been reminded by Benjamin scholarship of the general fact that many of his literary and philosophical reflections, whether they concern such matters as history, memory, art or technology, turn on his evocations of concrete objects, 'old and used, neglected and buried, dusty and hidden, broken and repaired'.[25] Such things in Benjamin's texts include, among many others, 'objects of daily use, commodities, garbage, children's toys, socks, telephones, glass shards, bottle openers, [and] antiques'.[26] By the same token, the omnipresence of objects among Benjamin's own words also leads him to become a reader of literature who is especially sensitive to the abiding presence of objects among the words of authors such as Kafka, Proust, Robert Walser, Franz Hessel and Louis Aragon.[27] It is therefore no accident that the children rummaging through the debris in the thought-image 'Construction Site' from *One-Way Street* emerge as secret revolutionaries of a politically saturated modernist montage, subjects for whom it is precisely in their relation to the discarded objects of modernity ('they feel irresistibly drawn to debris') that they come to encounter 'the face that the world of things turns especially to them and them alone [*das Gesicht, das die Dingwelt gerade ihnen, ihnen allein, zukehrt*]'.[28] And when it comes to a thing such as the telephone, an object that Benjamin in the *Berlin Chronicle* strategically calls his 'twin', the textual imbrication of thingliness, thinking, selfhood and critique even functions as one of the primal scenes of his entire autobiographical corpus.[29]

But it is in the *Arcades Project* that he provides a number of sustained conceptual insights into the material and theoretical relation to things first broached in the Goethe essay. While the figure that Benjamin emphasizes in the *Arcades Project* is often that of the collector – especially in Convolutes H and I – the general points he advances also can be said to apply to the critic and to the relation between critique and thing. It is in the context of a massive theoretical and historiographic effort that critique and thing are made to speak to each other. As in so many other regards, Baudelaire is enlisted as Benjamin's crown witness: 'One must make one's way through *Les Fleurs du mal* with a sense for how things are raised to allegory [*wie die Dinge zur Allegorie erhoben werden*]. The use of the uppercase lettering should be followed carefully.'[30] The thing emerges as thoroughly allegorical, even when it consists of the materiality of the letter in Baudelaire. If the thing is elevated to the level of allegory, it is made to speak *otherwise*, representing not only itself, its appearance as and in form, but also that which within it remains unspoken and unthought.

If critique is to confront the double nature of the thing, it is called upon to fashion perspectives that would do justice to the requirements of the critical act in relation to the position and presentation of the thing. As Benjamin argues:

> The true method of making things present to oneself [*die Dinge sich gegenwärtig zu machen*] is to present them in our space (not to present ourselves in their space) … . Thus presented, the things allow no mediating construction from out of 'larger contexts.' The same applies to the viewing of great things from the past—the cathedral of Chartres, the temple of Peastum—when, that is, a favorable prospect presents itself: to receive the things in our space. We do not put ourselves into their place; they step into our life [*Nicht wir versetzen uns in sie, sie treten in unser Leben*].[31]

To relate to a thing on the rigorous level of critique requires that one tear it out of its 'own' context, shunning all the surrounding elements that are assumed to provide meaning. This method is not one of empathy, in which the critic enters the space and context of the thing in order to comment upon the ways in which it looks like, or does not look like, the other things inhabiting its orbit. On the contrary, to relate to a thing in this Benjaminian way is to perform a certain kind of violence, in which the provenance of a thing is robbed of the aura of its naturalness and in which the rightful positionality – and therefore assumed meaning – of a thing is dis-placed with an eye

toward recontextualizing it in a critical constellation that is quite
alien to it. The moment in which the thing enters the space of being-
in-the-world, when it encroaches and even intrudes, it no longer can
be held at a safe distance. It is only now, in this unsettling moment of
having been encroached upon, that a critique of the thing is moved
to question its own methodological procedures and to reinvent itself
in accordance with the strange singularity and incommensurate
idiomaticity of the thing that has arrived. Benjamin's passage, finally,
also reverberates with an earlier one from 'The Return of the Flaneur',
a review of Hessel, in which he quotes Hessel's remarkable words
'We see only what looks at us [*Nur was uns anschaut sehen wir*]'
in a gesture that implies a complex reversal of the directionality of
looking conventionally believed to be obtained between humans and
things.[32] Here, it is precisely the thing staring at us that causes it to
step into our field of vision.[33]

We might say that it is according to this particular logic of
a thing looking at us and stepping toward us that one of the
dimensions of what Benjamin, in the section of his dissertation
on German Romanticism that investigates the relation between
the Early Romantic theory of art and Goethe, calls 'criticizability'
(*Kritisierbarkeit*) is cast into exacting relief. He writes: 'The concept
of a critique of art ... itself bespeaks an unambiguous dependence on
the center of the philosophy of art. This dependence is most acutely
formulated in the problem of the criticizability of the artwork ... .
The entire art-philosophical project of the early Romantics therefore
can be summarized by saying that they sought to demonstrate in
principle the criticizability of the work of art.'[34] While the specific
thing that Benjamin here connects to criticizability is the aesthetically mediated realm of the artwork, the speculative investment in
criticizability also can be extended to a larger, more encompassing
Dingwelt. That is to say, if his concern is with articulating a rigorous
concept of criticizability, it must unfold in relation to something, to

some thing, that allows the act of critique to become not simply the
execution of a pre-established agenda or a methodological doctrine
but rather the manifestation of the idea of a potentiality, an as yet
unpredictable, future-oriented critical attitude. This potentiality of
the act of critique is encoded in the suffix '–ability' (*-ierbarkeit*). As
Samuel Weber has shown in his recent study of the numerous terms
ending in '–ability' that traverse Benjamin's entire corpus (including
criticizability, reproducibility, translatability, citability, legibility and
impartibility, among many others), Benjamin is concerned with a
certain *virtuality* of writing and thinking, one that emphasizes radical
possibility over achieved actuality.[35] We can now add that the criticizability of a thing depends on the ways in which it presents itself to the
critic – rather than the critic entering the orbit of the thing – in a way
that works to keep possibility alive even in a thing, that is, even in the
realm of something whose meaning and function already appear to
have been decided upon by virtue of its having assumed a particular
shape and determined position in the *Dingwelt*.

If Benjamin emphasizes the moments of potentiality and possibility
in relation to a critique of the thing, his critical gesture also implies
that the thing cannot simply be assumed to remain self-identical
and fully transparent to the linguistically mediated consciousness
with which it interacts. We could say that Benjamin here provides a
reinterpretation and actualization of Hegel's discussion of the thing in
the section on consciousness entitled 'Sense-Certainty: Or the "This"
and "Meaning" [*Meinen*]' from *The Phenomenology of Spirit*. There,
Hegel writes:

> They speak of the existence [*Dasein*] of *external* objects [*Gegenstände*],
> which can be more precisely defined as *actual*, absolutely *singular*,
> *wholly personal*, *individual* things [*Dinge*], each of them absolutely
> unlike anything else; this existence, they say, has absolute certainty
> and truth. They mean *this* bit of paper on which I am writing—or
> rather have written—*this*; but what they mean is not what they say. If

they actually wanted to *say* 'this' bit of paper which they mean, if they
wanted to *say* it, then this is impossible, because the sensuous This that
is meant *cannot be reached* by language [*der Sprache ... unerreichbar
ist*], which belongs to consciousness, i.e. to that which is inherently
universal... . If nothing more is said of something than that it is an
actual thing [*ein wirkliches Ding*], an *external object*, its description is
only the most general and in fact expresses its sameness with everything rather than its difference.[36]

To confront the *Dinge* and *Gegenstände* upon which it fastens,
consciousness, along with the language that mediates it, is called
upon to show itself responsible to the ways in which its inscription
in the perpetual dialectic of particularity and universality inflects the
manner in which a thing can be thought and spoken about in the
first place. While in his lecture course on aesthetics Hegel emphasizes
that the concept, as something universal and intangible, needs the
manifestation of the particular in order to make it concrete, here his
argumentation proceeds in the other direction, as it were: Because
consciousness by virtue of language is always already indebted to a
sign system of universal signification, it cannot ever quite account for
the singularity and idiomaticity of *this thing*, which shares its designation with so many other things like it.

In the section of the *Phenomenology* entitled 'Perception: Or
the Thing and Deception [*Die Wahrnehmung oder das Ding und
die Täuschung*]', Hegel therefore proposes the following dialectical
account of the thing: 'The Thing is a *One* [*Das Ding ist* Eins], reflected
into itself; it is *for itself*, but it is also *for an other*; that is to say, it is an
other on its own account, just because it is for an other. Accordingly,
the Thing is for itself and *also* for an other, a being that is doubly
differentiated but also a One.'[37] Training the focus of his general
discussion of the for-oneself and the for-another on the particular
question of thing, Hegel opens up a dialectical space in which to
consider the thing as something that is at once unified enough to be

recognizable as a thing – as *this* thing or as *that* thing – and traversed by a certain nonself-identity in which it vacillates between a self-referential determinant (being for itself) and an other-directed entity (being for another). One of the questions posed by this dialectical self-differentiation of the thing concerns its availability to a critical consciousness, which also must, in the critical act, take into account this radically dialectical movement. If Benjamin wishes to develop a concept of critique that travels through an engagement with the thing, it is in part because of the Hegelian inheritance that complicates any interrogation of the thing, and even the thingness of the thing. What a Benjaminian criticizability of the thing therefore also would have to entail is a consideration of how a thing can become an object of critique when it no longer merely is an object, that is, when it no longer will remain an effect of the subject-object split and of a perspective that assumes it to be transparently available to critical consciousness. This, too, is why for Benjamin the things inhabiting the *Dingwelt* 'step toward us', as he puts it, *treten in unser Leben*, as unfinished business.

For Benjamin's idea of critique, in which the critic becomes a physiognomist of the *Dingwelt*, the thing's hermeneutic instability embodies simultaneously the predicament of post-lapsarian, secularized modernity itself. We recall that in his *Trauerspiel* book, *The Origin of the German Mourning Play*, Benjamin provocatively suggests that on the Baroque stage, which, for him, can be read as an allegory of modernity as such, 'any person, any thing [*jedwedes Ding*], any relation can mean absolutely anything else [*kann ein beliebiges anderes bedeuten*]'.[38] This separation of sign and signification is not simply a liberation from the strictures of a prematurely imposed stable meaning, it also is a cause for mourning. This mourning, for Benjamin, is anchored in the world of things. The fidelity or faithfulness that traverses this particular form of mourning cannot be thought in isolation from the ways in which it is directed not to a

person or an idea but rather to a thing. Speaking of the figure of the
courtier in the mourning play, Benjamin states:

> His infidelity [*Untreue*] to the human being corresponds to a fidelity
> [*Treue*] to these things to the point of being absorbed in contemplative
> devotion to them. Only in this hopeless fidelity to the creaturely ...
> does the concept of this behavior stand in the location of its adequate
> fulfilment. For, all essential decisions before human beings can violate
> fidelity; in them, higher laws obtain. Fidelity is fully appropriate only
> to the relation between the human being and the world of things
> [*Dingwelt*]. The latter knows no higher law, and fidelity knows no
> object to which it might belong more exclusively than the world of
> things ... . Melancholy betrays the world for the sake of knowledge.
> But in its tenacious sunkenness [*ausdauernde Versunkenheit*] it admits
> dead things into its contemplation [*nimmt die toten Dinge in ihre
> Kontemplation auf*] in order to redeem them ... . The persistence that
> takes shape in the intention of mourning is born of its fidelity to the
> world of things.[39]

To the extent that the critical act – especially the one involving an
allegorical reading, which, for Benjamin, is the preferred mode in
the *Trauerspiel* book and in his theory of reading more generally –
is capable of being informed by a certain fidelity, it can only be a
fidelity that pertains to an interpretation of the perpetually shifting
relations between human and thing. Even the cardinal sin of melancholia – betraying the world in exchange for the fruits of *Wissen*
– is reconfigured when seen from this perspective. Like the winged
figure dispassionately staring at the manifold things that surround
it in Albrecht Dürer's famous allegorical woodcut 'Melancholia', the
melancholic critic opens the space of reflection to the dead things,
displaying a certain hospitality toward them, and even making
them the focus of his reflections.[40] In this act of critique, the thing
in a certain sense appears as both dead and alive: dead, because it
belongs merely to the dead *Dingwelt* as an inanimate, mute entity;
alive, because it enters into critical contemplation (*'nimmt die toten*

Dinge ... auf') in yet another act of what Benjamin calls the thing's 'stepping toward us'. We might say that this movement of the thing is one of Benjamin's responses to the Hegelian challenge of having to regard *das Ding* both as something self-referential and as something other-directed, as an object readily available to critique and as a dialectical phenomenon that works to elude its critic's gaze. The thing becomes, we might say, part of the realm of what Benjamin terms *das Ausdruckslose*, the expressionless, a moment or realm that is cognizable as some-thing but that refuses to provide a hermeneutic key to itself.[41] It must, as it were, be inherited *otherwise*.

III.

Let us now turn to Heidegger's inheritance. It is an open question to what extent Heidegger's project, which is concerned with the end of metaphysics and the exhaustion of traditional – especially institutional – modes of philosophy, can be said to participate in the heritage of critique at all. It is perhaps telling that one looks in vain for entries on 'critique' in today's standard reference works of Heidegger scholarship.[42] And from the perspective of critique understood as a form of historical materialism, it is as though many readers and scholars had accepted the logic of Heidegger's former student Herbert Marcuse, who had completed his doctoral thesis on Hegel's theory of historicity under Heidegger's direction, and who, after an initial attempt to bring Heideggerian thought and Marxian critique together, abandoned the project of a 'Heideggerian Marxism' as impossible.[43] And yet, especially the relation between critique and the materiality of a thing – a relation that concerns Heidegger as much as it does Benjamin – would still deserve to be analysed with comparative reference to a Marxian notion of materialism. After all, in the 'Letter on "Humanism"', Heidegger, in a rare reference to

Marx, suggests a certain link between his concern with submitting to critique the ways in which the question of Being has been occluded and the Marxian critique of estrangement:

> What Marx, coming from Hegel, recognized in an essential and significant sense as the alienation of the human being has its roots in the homelessness of the modern human being. This homelessness is specifically evoked from the destiny of Being in the form of metaphysics, and through metaphysics is simultaneously fortified and covered up as such. Because Marx, by experiencing alienation, reaches into an essential dimension of history, the Marxist view of history is superior [*überlegen*] to that of other historical accounts. But since neither Husserl nor—so far as I have seen until now—Sartre recognizes the essential importance of the historical in Being, neither phenomenology nor existentialism enters that dimension within which a productive dialogue with Marxism first becomes possible.[44]

The implication of these lines is not only that there may be much stronger affinities than is commonly assumed between, on the one hand, Heideggerian concepts of ontological historicity in which the commemorative thinking of modes of Being have been repressed, and, on the other hand, the repression that is given voice in Marxian materialism, but they also suggest that questions concerning Marx's critique of the reified thing in terms of its embodiment of commodity fetishism would here join concerns over the ontological assumption that human beings and the being of things has been occluded in favour of a superficial rationalism. By the same token, these lines also cast the project of rehabilitating the thinking of Being as, *among other things*, a critical and material intervention into ossified ways of thinking and acting, that is, as a form of critique.

To be sure, if post-Kantian critique, even in its transformations through Hegel and Marx, can, from a certain perspective, be considered to be one of the primary preoccupations of metaphysical speculation, then it would appear problematic to ascribe a *critical* component to a project that is more concerned with the truth of *aletheia*, or unconcealment, than with any truth-content of critique. And yet, careful readers of Heideggerian ontology and of the post-Kantian tradition of critique have begun to intuit that there is more of a relation between the existentialist path of thinking and the post-Kantian concept of critique than may at first be obvious. It has been convincingly argued, for instance, that the basic orientation of *Being and Time* is precisely to conjoin a properly critical attitude in the area of epistemology to a fundamental reconsideration of *Dasein* as an unthought mode of being-in-the-world. 'Construing *Dasein* as being-in-the-world (marked by care for being)', the political theorist Fred Dallmayr reminds us, 'did not signal a return to a pre-critical or substantive metaphysics', but revealed, in 'its basic anti-objectivism', that 'fundamental ontology was not alien to, but rather a precondition of possible critique—though a critique cognizant of its underpinnings and limitations'.[45] From this vantage, 'Heidegger's work can be seen as a primary exemplar of a perspective combining ontological reflection with post-Kantian (not subject-centered) critique'.[46] According to the demands of this critique, even a reflection on *Dasein* must be a form of critical *self-reflection*, even when it takes certain elements of post-Kantian rationalism to task for its occlusion of what Heidegger regards as the more primordial question – the question of Being.

It is Heidegger himself, for instance in his 1964 lecture 'The End of Philosophy and the Task of Thinking' – one of his most significant statements regarding his vision for a rigorous thinking yet to come – who explicitly relates this thinking to the critical act. Whereas philosophy in its classical, metaphysical sense is concerned with providing answers to questions, what is needed is a different kind of thinking, one that emphasizes the importance of the path (*der Weg*) and that takes into account what has remained unthought. Heidegger writes: 'Questions are paths toward an answer. If the answer could be given it would consist in a transformation of thinking, not in a propositional statement about a matter at stake.' Suggesting that his text belongs to a larger attempt at articulating the question of Being in an even 'more primordial fashion' than that of *Being and Time*, the task can be outlined as follows:

> This means to subject the point of departure of the question in *Being and Time* to an immanent critique [*Kritik*]. Thus it must become clear to what extent the *critical* question [*die* kritische *Frage*], as to what the matter of thinking is, necessarily and continually belongs to thinking. Accordingly, the name of the task of *Being and Time* will change.[47]

Whereas *Being and Time* had articulated its tasks in terms of an anthropologically mediated ontology rather than of critique, Heidegger now regards the future of actual thinking, rather than merely 'doing' philosophy, as being tied to the question of critique, even italicizing the adjective '*kritisch*' to make his point. The work of critique here is conceptualized not primarily as a mode of external intervention, that is, as a movement of separation between entities that are assumed already to exist as a form of presence and self-identity. Rather, critique is a mode of thinking about the very acts of questioning, even of the idea of the question itself. Therefore, Heidegger speaks not simply of critique but rather of a 'kritische *Frage*'.

What this questioning pursued by the 'kritische *Frage*' entails cannot be thought in isolation from a consideration of the ways in which it differs from classical metaphysics. Heidegger explains: 'All metaphysics, including its opponent, positivism, speaks the language of Plato. The basic word of its thinking, that is, of its presentation of the Being of beings [*das Sein des Seienden*], is *eidos*, idea: the outward appearance in which beings as such show themselves.' He adds: 'Outward appearance, however, is a matter of presence.'[48] What is needed to cognize any presence, even the presence of the *eidos*, is the light provided by a sudden clearing (*Lichtung*) that traverses Being but nevertheless has tended to remain 'unthought' (*ungedacht*) in Western philosophy. To approach the unthought by means of the 'kritische *Frage*' means above all to break with the convention of translating the Greek *aletheia* as truth, carrying it into the realm of the critical question by rendering it as unconcealment. As Heidegger argues:

> *Aletheia*, unconcealment thought as the clearing of presence, is not yet truth. Is *aletheia* less than truth? Or is it more, because it first grants truth as *adaequatio* and *certitudo*, because there can be no presence and presenting outside the realm of the clearing?
>
> This question we leave to thinking as a task. Thinking must consider [*muß sich darauf besinnen*] whether it can even pose this question at all as long as it thinks philosophically, that is, in the strict sense of metaphysics, which questions what is present only with regard to its presence.[49]

What is disclosed in the critical question is that we still do not know how to think, are still in need of an understanding of thinking. The unconcealment that facilitates our cognition of the changed status of truth in the task of thinking is itself the commencement of an education in thinking, a thinking that perpetually questions its own assumptions. The thinking (*das Denken*) yet to come pursues previously untrodden paths and fosters forms of contemplative vigilance and attentiveness with regard to what had hitherto remained unthought in metaphysics. 'The task of thinking', in Heidegger's view, 'would then be the surrender of previous thinking to the determination of the matter of thinking.'[50] This determination is inseparable from certain modes of interpreting the status of the 'kritische *Frage*'.

As in the case of Benjamin's development of critique, it is through constant dialogue, explicit or implicit, with the Kantian formulation of critique that Heidegger's own engagement with the 'kritische *Frage*' unfolds. The question and the questioning of critique in Kant's enterprise have not settled a priori on an assumed negativity of critique. In the *Critique of Pure Reason*, Kant writes:

What sort of treasure is it that we intend to leave to posterity, in the form of a metaphysics that has been purified through critique but therefore also brought into a changeless state? On a cursory overview … one might believe that one perceives it to be only of *negative* utility, teaching us never to venture with speculative reason beyond the boundaries of experience; and in fact that is its first usefulness. But this utility becomes *positive* when we become aware that the principles with which speculative reason ventures beyond its boundaries do not in fact result in *extending* our use of reason … . Hence a critique that limits the speculative use of reason is, to be sure, to that extent *negative*, but because it simultaneously removes an obstacle that limits or even threatens to wipe out the practical use of reason, this critique is also in fact of *positive* and very important utility … . To deny that this service of critique is of any *positive* utility would be as much as to say that the police are of no positive utility because their chief business is to put a stop to the violence that citizens have to fear from other citizens, so that each can carry on his own affairs in peace and safety.[51]

The question regarding the negativity or positivity of critique strikes at the core of the concept of a transcendental, critical philosophy. Here, the radicality of Kant's concept of critique does not just lie in the fact that his transcendental method accords it a functional value that was without precedent in what Kant himself had already referred to as an age of critique.[52] The true radicality of his concept of critique lies instead in its extension to the self-critique of reason on the far side of critique as posited negativity. Reason here must also submit itself to the demands of critique if it is to arrive at self-knowledge. It must learn, as Rodolphe Gasché reminds us, not only to think of its criteria and boundaries through the aspect of critique, but to establish critique as the gold standard of its own chief enterprise.[53] We recall, therefore, that post-Kantian critique is at the same time to be a critical theory of itself, a type of contemplation that turns away from all dogmas and forms of mere scepticism to make the radicality of self-reflection the principle of every critical movement of thought.

In paragraph 21 of Chapter 2 in *Die Frage nach dem Ding*
(literally, 'The Question Concerning the Thing' or 'The [Status of the]
Question After the Thing' and published in English under the title
What Is a Thing?), a text based on a lecture course on Kant held in
Freiburg during the winter semester of 1935–6, Heidegger pursues
the question: 'What does "Critique" mean in Kant?' He writes:
'We are accustomed to hearing something overwhelmingly negative
whenever this word is mentioned. For us, to criticize means to find
fault, to tally mistakes, to point out shortcomings, and to dismiss
what is thereby found wanting. We must try to distance ourselves
from this customary and misleading meaning when faced with the
title *Critique of Pure Reason*.'[54] Heidegger continues:

> 'Critique' comes from the Greek *krinein*, which means 'to sort'
> [*sondern*], 'to sort out,' and thus 'to lift out that special sort' [*das
> Besondere herausheben*] … . 'Critique,' far from being something
> negative, designates the most positive positivity, the positing of what
> must be put in place before everything else as the determining and
> decisive agency. Critique is thus decision in this pre-positional sense.
> Only in consequence of this, because to criticize means to select and to
> bring out what is special, uncommon, and at the same time measure-
> giving, is it also to reject what is commonplace and unsuitable.[55]

We should note that if Heidegger associates with critique nothing
negative but rather 'the most positive positivity', we cannot but hear
echoes of Benjamin's inheritance of critique along positive rather
than negative lines: 'Thus, critique, in complete opposition to the
present-day conception of its essence, is, in its central intention, not
judgment but, on the one hand, the completion, supplementation,
and systematization of the work and, on the other hand, its disso-
lution in the absolute.'[56] Critique, for both Benjamin and Heidegger,
is not primarily the negation of something but its radical affirmation,
a way of accentuating what is distinct and singular in an argument, a
mode of discourse, or a work.

Heidegger proceeds to provide historical texture to this systematic view of the workings of critique by arguing that the general meaning of the word 'critique' gradually takes shape in the second half of the eighteenth century in discussions of art, the analysis of artistic forms and the promulgation of rules and decrees. 'But the word', Heidegger adds, 'receives a fuller sense through Kant's work.'[57] It is incumbent on thought, according to this view, to understand this fuller meaning. 'If critique has this positive meaning', he remarks, 'then the *Critique of Pure Reason* will not simply dismiss and rebuke pure reason, "criticize" it, but will instead first set out to circumscribe its decisive, peculiar, and hence proper being. This act of circumscription is not primarily one of preventative foreclosure [*Abgrenzung gegen*], but rather one of enclosure [*Eingrenzung*], in the sense that it demonstrates the inner articulation of pure reason.'[58] From this situation, the conclusion could be drawn that critique is not simply 'censorship'. Referring to Leibniz and Baumgarten, Heidegger adds that one would be equally mistaken to regard 'the architectonics, the architectural plan of the essential structure of pure reason', as 'mere "display"'.[59] From the perspective of fundamental ontology, a concept of critique interpreted in this way would help to determine the essence of reason itself.

This determination would need to be thought in relation to the opposing figures of foreclosure and enclosure, *Ab-grenzung* and *Ein-grenzung*. If the self-reflexive gesture of critique is one of *Eingrenzung* rather than of *Abgrenzung*, as Heidegger claims almost in passing, then *Abgrenzung* could be seen as a defensive ploy, a self-defensive measure directed by critical thought against an other that threatens to hinder its movement from outside, as it were. The *Eingrenzung* performed by critique, by contrast, remains in principle open to the influence of that other, whether that influence be friendly or hostile, since unlike *Abgrenzung* it does not seek to expel it as a persistent danger. The *Eingrenzung* of critique is far more preoccupied with its own procedures, cognitive schemata and unexpressed assumptions; indeed, it seeks its most radical fulfilment in the interminable determination of its own assumptions and in their critique. In this sense, critique wants nothing more than to criticize itself; that is to say, it would first come to itself by interrogating and hence potentially taking leave of itself. Such *Eingrenzung*, in contrast to *Abgrenzung*, would at the same time also have to be conceived as a potentiality, a state in which agreement on its own assumptions and inferential models remains still to come.

It is now time to take seriously Heidegger's statement that 'even this understanding is only in the service of an insight into the question "What is a thing?" [*dient nur der Einsicht in die Frage: "Was ist ein Ding?"*]' by turning toward the speculative field in which this Heideggerian engagement with the movement of Kantian critique finds expression, namely, in his thinking about the thing.[60] In the First Critique Kant speaks of 'the distinction between things [*Dinge*] as objects of experience and the very same things as things in themselves, which our critique has made necessary', linking the concept of critique to a consideration of the thing in a manner that will not elude Heidegger.[61] Yet what are the relays between critique and the question concerning the thing in Heidegger's project? As Heidegger's student Walter Biemel reminds us, Heidegger's task as outlined already in *Being and Time* is to inquire into the essence of the beings that surround us in our quotidian life-world. But even when Heidegger addresses such everyday things as chairs and hammers, his aim is not to provide any kind of 'picture-book phenomenology' of things that are already familiar but rather to think toward the ways in which our relation to things inflects how we inhabit the world in and as our *Dasein* via particular and often unthought modes of being.[62] While Heidegger's interest in the question of the thing in the aftermath of Kantian critique traverses much of his thought, it receives some of its most explicit treatments in certain passages of

Being and Time (1927, especially paragraphs 15 and 16), in the Kant book *Die Frage nach dem Ding* (based on a 1935–6 Freiburg lecture course and first published in 1962), in the 1936 essay 'The Origin of the Work of Art', and in the later essays 'Das Ding' ('The Thing') and 'Building Dwelling Thinking' (1950–1).

We might say, first of all, that it is not a mere contingency of discursive organization that Heidegger's analysis of critique as the most positive positivity is embedded in a consideration of the logic of transcendental principles as they relate to the question of the thing in Kant. In Section B of *Die Frage nach dem Ding*, entitled 'Kant's Manner of Asking About the Thing', we read that what is essential in 'the philosophical determination of the thingness of the thing which Kant has created' is 'not an accidental by-product'; rather, 'the determination of the thingness of the thing is its metaphysical center. By means of an interpretation [*Auslegung*] of Kant's work we put ourselves on the path of the inherently historical question concerning the thing.'[63] It is interesting to note that Heidegger here uses the word *Auslegung* instead of the word derived from Latin, *Interpretation*, which also is commonly used in German. *Aus-legung* literally is a laying-out, a placing before oneself, of the elements that comprise the matter calling for understanding. As such, an *Aus-legung*, as a laying-out, retains, at least to a German ear, the imagery of actual things being presented in a concrete, almost haptic sense. For Heidegger, approaching the question of Kantian critique through an investigation of the thingness of the thing is a way of inhabiting Kant's thought from the inside, as it were. He writes: 'We turn our question "What is a thing?" into Kant's and, vice versa, Kant's question into ours ... We need not report in broad surveys and general phrases "about" the philosophy of Kant. We put ourselves within it.'[64] This mode of dwelling in Kant's thought, in his way of inventing the modern concept of critique, is what also should give rise to a questioning of the thing. For Heidegger, this becomes evident already in a consideration of the title of Kant's First Critique:

Critique of Pure Reason—everyone knows what 'critique' and 'to criticize' mean; 'reason' and what a 'reasonable' man or a 'reasonable' suggestion is, are also understood by everyone. What 'pure' signifies in distinction to impure (e.g., impure water) is clear also. Yet we cannot think anything appropriate to the title, *Critique of Pure Reason*. Above all, one would expect a critique to reject something unsatisfactory, insufficient, and negative; one would expect criticism of something like impure reason. Finally, it is quite incomprehensible what the *Critique of Pure Reason* can have to do with the question concerning the thing. And yet we are completely justified in asserting that this title expresses nothing else but the question concerning the thing—but as a question. The question is, as we know, historical. The title means this history in a decisive era of its movement. The title means this question, and it is a thoroughly historical one. In an external sense this means that Kant, who was thoroughly clear about his work, gave it a title demanded by his age and, at the same time, led beyond it. What history of the question concerning the thing is expressed in this title?[65]

To pursue the question of the thing that emerged from a consideration of critique, Heidegger interrogates the logic of categories as modes of assertion, such as quality, relation, time and place. This interrogation leads him to assert that the thinking about the thingness of the thing and its truth are to be found not simply in the material there-ness of the object, but in certain principles of pure reason. According to the Kantian scheme as interpreted by Heidegger, 'the pure inner lawfulness of reason, from out of its fundamental principles and concepts, decides about the being of what is, the thingness of things' based on a series of principles (including the principle of contradiction and the principle of sufficient reason, among others) that can be schematized and formalized through an act of reason's self-constitution. It is here that pure reason becomes 'the authoritative court of appeal for the determination of the thingness of all things as such—it is this pure reason which Kant places into "critique"'.[66] In short, we could say that Heidegger's argument is that if critique for Kant is the self-knowledge of pure reason, then it is the question of the thing, even the thingness of the thing, that determines the principles according to which an act of understanding is grounded in a mode of reflective judgement.

While Heidegger lays out the general relation between critique and the thing in his engagement with Kant, a more detailed interrogation of the vexing question of the thingness of the thing is carried out in 'The Origin of the Work of Art'. There, distancing himself from conventional views of the thing – as substance characterized by determinable characteristics, as the unifying term with which mind organizes the multiplicity of its sensory data and as the form of matter that is shaped into cognizable form – he advances a notion of the thing that unfolds on the far side of its tool-likeness or its mere equipment-character. To choose this path is, for Heidegger, to be invited to the table of 'the feast of thinking [*das Fest des Denkens*], assuming that thinking is a craft [*das Denken ein Handwerk ist*].'[67] Reminding us of the thingliness of even the most rarefied work of art, Heidegger writes: 'The picture hangs on the wall like a hunting rifle or a hat. A painting, e.g., the one by Van Gogh that represents a pair of peasant shoes, travels from one exhibition to the other. Works are shipped like coal from the Ruhr and logs from the Black Forest.' He continues: 'During the war Hölderlin's hymns were packed in the soldier's knapsack together with cleaning gear. Beethoven's quartets lie in the storerooms of the publishing house like potatoes in a cellar.'[68] But Heidegger's point is not to reduce the work of art to its thingness, however conceptualized, if by the thing's thingness is meant only its conventional interpretations. That is to say, the point is not to perpetuate the concept of the thing as all that appears, as all that is and that is *as such* – Heidegger mentions such things as the stone in the road, the thistle in the field, the cloud in the sky, the leaf in the autumn breeze, the jug, the airplane and the radio – but rather to differentiate the general realm of beings (*das Seiende*) from the mode of Being proper to a thing.

In order to understand this Heideggerean argument, we might say that a careful approach to this dimension of the thing as *Ding* also would entail its differentiation from contiguous determinations, including other German words for 'thing' such as *Gegenstand* (literally, a 'standing-against'), *das Objekt*, and *die Sache*. In the area of psychoanalysis, for instance, Jacques Lacan in his seminars reminds us to distinguish between *das Ding* and *die Sache* when we approach the far-reaching consequences of the relation that Freud posits between the pleasure principle and the gestures of sublimation.[69] But the particular kind of distinction that Heidegger wishes to make here is that between *Ding* and *Zeug*, understood as the shaped material used as a kind of equipment. 'The equipmental being of equipment [*Zeugsein des Zeuges*],' Heidegger argues, 'reliability, keeps gathered within itself all things according to their manner and extent. The usefulness of equipment is nevertheless only the essential consequence of reliability. The former vibrates in the latter and would be nothing without it. A single piece of equipment is worn out and used up; but at the same time the use itself also falls into disuse, wears away, and becomes usual.'[70] But precisely this predominance of the equipment-character of beings is what needs to be called into question in order to appreciate more fully the essence of the thingness of the thing. The space of the work of art is delimited by its contiguity with both the realm of the *Zeug* and the realm of the *Ding*. The crux of Heidegger's reflections here is that what 'matters is a first opening of our field of vision to the fact that what is workly in the work, equipmental in equipment, and thingly in the thing comes closer to us only when we think the Being of beings [*das Sein des Seienden denken*]'. Yet this opening up does not mean that a consideration of the thingness of the work of art leads us to a determination of that work, as if the thinking of the thingness of the thing could be instrumentalized, and then presumably discarded, in the service of ascertaining the alleged meaning of a work. For

Heidegger, if unconcealment takes shape in the work of art, 'then the road toward the determination of the thingly reality of the work leads not from thing to work but from work to thing'.[71] The question concerning the thing therefore remains uncannily open, resistant to being instrumentalized in the service of this or that regime wishing to dominate the world of beings.

Heidegger's 1950 talk 'The Thing' inflects his concern with the thingness of the thing found in the Kant lecture and in the artwork essay in new ways. Specifically, the text situates the question concerning the thing in relation to his other speculative preoccupations at the time: the uncanny fulfilment and closure of Western metaphysics through modern technics ('The Question Concerning Technology', 1953), the meaning of thinking under such conditions ('What Is Called Thinking', 1952), and the problem regarding the relationship between how one dwells and how one thinks ('Building Dwelling Thinking' as well as ' … Poetically Man Dwells … ', 1951). It pursues intricate questions concerning the thing's relation to the disappearance of the experience of distance and proximity in the age of global travel and telecommunication; to the scientific view of the thing as a matter of physical describability; to the experience of a gathering; and, perhaps most mystifying, to the fourfold (*das Geviert*), the name that Heidegger bestows on his ontological constellation of mortals, Gods, heaven and earth. Unlike Plato's view of all that is present as a matter of prior manufacture and of its mode of appearance, Heidegger focuses on the ways in which a thing exists as a such-and-such, that is, on the as-ness of the thing as it discloses itself as a form of presence. Asking about the particular thingliness of the thing, he provides the example of a jug (*der Krug*) and the manifold ways of looking at its being-as-a-thing, submitting to scrutiny the numerous ways of looking at a drinking vessel, none of which ultimately satisfy. The crux of the difficulties in ascertaining the thingness of the jug for Heidegger is lodged at the core of the insight that 'no presentation of what is present [*Vorstellung des Anwesenden*], in the sense of what stands forth and of what stands over against as an object [*im Sinne des Herständigen und Gegenständlichen*], ever reaches to the thing *qua* thing [*gelangt jedoch nie zum Ding als Ding*]. The jug's thingness resides in its being *qua* vessel.' Heidegger continues:

> We become aware of the vessel's holding nature [*das Fassende des Gefäßes*] when we fill the jug. The jug's bottom and sides obviously take on the task of holding. But not so fast! When we fill the jug with wine, do we pour the wine into the sides and bottom? At most, we pour the wine between the sides and over the bottom. Sides and bottom are, to be sure, what is impermeable in the vessel. But what is impermeable is not yet what does the holding. When we fill the jug, the pouring that fills it flows into the empty jug. The emptiness, the void, is what does the vessel's holding. The empty space, this nothing of the jug, is what the jug is as the holding vessel ... But if the holding is done by the jug's void, then the potter who forms sides and bottom on his wheel does not, strictly speaking, make the jug. He only shapes the clay. No—he shapes the void [*er gestaltet die Leere*] ... The vessel's thingness does not lie at all in the material of which it consists, but in the void that holds [*Das Dinghafte des Gefäßes beruht keineswegs im Stoff, daraus es besteht, sondern in der Leere, die faßt*].[72]

Heidegger's point is neither to challenge the laws of physics nor to assert the metaphysical nature of the thing. Rather, he wishes to question the narrowly conceived notion of scientific rationality that would reduce the thingness of the thing either to its physical qualities or to its mere existence as substance to be calculated according to predetermined measuring sticks. This scientific view ultimately leads to the erasure of thing as thing, that is, as a provocation to our received and proscribed modes of *Dasein*. For Heidegger, by contrast, once the questioning of the thingness of the thing commences, thinking the thing will not lead us to a stable determination of its essence but ever more deeply into a certain void, an obscurity of the unthought that perpetually calls for thinking.

This call for thinking cannot but engage the etymology of the very word and concept that are at stake here. Therefore, Heidegger clarifies the word-historical imbrications of the thing, summarizing his thoughts as follows:

> The Roman word *res* names that which concerns somebody, an affair, a contested matter, a case at law. The Romans also use for it the word *causa*. In its authentic and original sense, this word in a way signifies 'cause [*Ursache*]'; *causa* means the case [*den Fall*] and hence also that which is the case [*was der Fall ist*], in the sense that something comes to pass and becomes due. Only because *causa*, almost synonymously with *res*, means the case, can the word *causa* later come to mean cause, in the sense of the causality of an effect. The Old High German word *thing* or *dinc*, with its meaning of a gathering specifically for the purpose of dealing with a case or matter, is suited as no other word to translate the Roman word *res*, that which is pertinent, which has a bearing. From that word of the Roman language, which corresponds to the word *res*—from the word *causa* in the sense of case, affair, matter of pertinence—there develop in turn the Romance *la cosa* and the French *la chose*; we say *das Ding*. In English *thing* has still preserved the full semantic power of the Roman word: 'He knows his things,' he understands the matters that have a bearing on him; 'he knows how to handle things,' he knows how to go about dealing with affairs, that is, with what matters from case to case; 'that's a great thing,' that is something grand (fine, tremendous, splendid), something that comes of itself bears upon the human being.[73]

But crucially, for Heidegger, the Romans left important features of the thing and its essential or primordial aspects unthought, bestowing upon the history of Western metaphysics a reductive perspective on the thingness of the thing that even the German mystic Meister Eckhart and, later, Kant and his engagement with the thing-in-itself (*Ding-an-sich*), could not fully overcome. Ultimately, according to this account, the task that presents itself to thinking is inflected by the view that the thing 'things', '*das Ding dingt*', and that the very thing that the thing things is world. This world is a matter of disclosure and unconcealment vis-à-vis the human *Dasein* that always already finds itself having been thrown into it, what in *Being and Time* is termed our human experience of existential *Geworfenheit*, or thrownness.

This kind of thinking of the thing that things world is also a question of coming and of vigilance. 'When and in what way do things come as things?', Heidegger asks, adding: 'They do not come *by means of* human making [*kommen nicht durch die Machenschaften des Menschen*]. But neither do they appear *without* the vigilance [*Wachsamkeit*] of mortals. The first step toward such vigilance is the step back from the thinking that merely represents—that is, explains— to the thinking that responds and recalls [*Der erste Schritt zu solcher Wachsamkeit ist der Schritt zurück aus dem nur vorstellenden, d.h. erklärenden Denken in das andenkende Denken*].'[74] Heidegger here conjoins his reflections on the thing with the most salient concerns of his later work. Rather than viewing philosophy as a metaphysical activity to be pursued by the mere machinations or obscure dealings (equally valid translations of *Machenschaften*) of human activity, thinking – both the thinking that considers the thing, and thinking more generally – no longer is to be tied to mere explanation, a scientific gesture that often explains away the unthought, rather than attempting to learn to think it.[75] Silently alluding to Hölderlin's poem 'Andenken', Heidegger's *andenkendes Denken* is a thinking that unfolds on the far side of mere calculation and rationalization. Rather, the vigilance that it performs – and *Wachsamkeit* will be a key operative concept for all of the later Heidegger – is both commemorative (*an etwas denken*) and constantly on the way somewhere else, somewhere that has not yet been reached as a destination (*andenken* as *denken an*). Like in his lecture 'Who Is Nietzsche's Zarathustra?' – presented in 1953, only a couple of years after 'The Thing' – Heidegger casts doubt on the claims made by both science (empiricism) and theology (belief) regarding what can be understood and experienced, instead focusing on facing a thinking kind of questioning that turns on what remains *fragwürdig*, questionable, or *frag-würdig*, worthy of being questioned. This thinking is, among other things, not a mere change in attitude, the adoption of a new method or recalibrated system. It is, rather, a tentative, probing, provisional questioning, even as it mediates upon the most obscure and fundamental issues of the unthought (*andenken* as *an-denken*, as a kind of initial thinking in the direction or according to the eventual possibility of something, as when one says in modern German, 'Wir haben es schon einmal angedacht', but still must concretize our plans and paths further). Uncompromising vigilance – at once haptic (like the jug) and speculative, commemorative and critical, inscribed in what has come to pass and persistently oriented toward a thinking yet to come – is the thinking that the thingness of the thing calls for.

IV.

Rainer Maria Rilke, a poet of significance to both Benjamin and Heidegger, and the author of what he famously called *Dinggedichte*, or 'thing-poems' – poems that allegorize particular things, such as a flower, while they themselves assumed the shape of language-as-thing – once confessed to Lou Andreas-Salomé that '*nur die Dinge reden zu mir* (only things speak to me)'.[76] Rilke makes this statement in the context of what one might call his 'thing letter', a missive that pivots on an analysis of Rodin's artistic way of dealing with the world of things. But in what ways can the thing in the world of things, artistic or otherwise, be made to speak? This question of making some-thing speak, making it tell us something that we did not already know, has provided the impetus for a broad span of artistic and scholarly experiments, from contemporary British artist Willard Wigan's exquisite microsculptures that fit in the eye of a

needle and often are made from dust fibers or tiny plastic slivers, via
John Sallis' remarkable meditation on the concept and experience
of stone, including mountains, writing tablets, towers, cathedrals,
temples and tombstones, all the way to Alphonso Lingis' poetically
inflected departures from conventional philosophies of mind toward
an understanding of our experience of the thingness of things in
terms of the specific kind of response that a thing elicits from an
embedded and bodily consciousness.[77]

How does the thing speak in and for Benjamin and Heidegger? If
the two writers, as the ones who are related in their non-relation, can
be thought together as each having worked toward a rearticulation
of the Kantian project of critique not by reverting to any form of
Neokantianism but rather by interlacing the concept of critique with
a consideration of the thingness of the thing, their methodological
perspectives emerge in a dual vision. For both thinkers, the form of
critique that is mobilized *in relation to* the thing – even when it is
not directed *at* the thing – proceeds by denaturalizing the contextual
determination that is conventionally reserved for a reading of things.
Both Benjamin and Heidegger require that the thing be torn out of
its assumed context – in Benjamin's case, the ossified constellation
of its historical embeddedness, and in Heidegger's case, the hidden
metaphysical assumptions about the things that present themselves
as beings – in order to become thinkable in a new way. While for
Benjamin a certain criticizability of the thing that encroaches upon
the allegedly familiar territory delimited by the critic's purview
names its status as a form of potentiality and futurity, for Heidegger
the thing qua thing refuses itself to the received standards according
to which Western thought relates our *Dasein* to our experiences of
a thing while it leaves the more difficult questions concerning the
thingness of the thing largely untouched. What calls for critique in
Benjamin's model is the very moment when the thing withdraws
from the transparency of its *Dingwelt* in order to step into our field of

vision and consciousness as an unanchored object, a piece of debris
that asks to be reinterpreted along with the cultural framework from
which it emerged. What calls for critique in the Heideggerian sense
is that moment when our uncompromising vigilance of thought can
no longer be reduced to the certainties of a philosophical tradition
in which the thing figures merely as an object exhibiting the laws of
physics or a certain set of scientifically describable qualities. We might
say that for both Benjamin and Heidegger, there remains something
unthought in both critique and the thing – unthought not in the sense
of an unfinished project that is as yet incomplete but in principle,
and with sufficient time and appropriate progress, is completable, but
rather in the sense that this unthought has remained obscure even
to the critic and therefore to the very ways in which questions about
an issue such as critique and the thing have been posed in the first
place. The thinking of critique via the thingness of the thing therefore
requires, in both the Benjaminian and Heideggerian models, a recalibration of the *question* that is meant to guide the unpredictable path
of our vigilant thinking.

While both Benjamin's and Heidegger's rearticulations of critique
via the question of the thing entertain certain parallels with powerful
contemporary revisions of critique such as Max Horkheimer's 1937
'Traditional and Critical Theory' – the first essay in Western thought
in which the term Critical Theory is used and discussed – their
projects do not fasten, like Horkheimer's, upon a revision of the
subject-object split that was inherited by bourgeois philosophy from
an overly narrow interpretation of Descartes' scientific method,
which is in turn extended to all forms of knowing to disastrous
effect.[78] Similarly, while both Benjamin and Heidegger, for all their
differences from each other and from Theodor W. Adorno, would
share the sentiment the latter expresses in his late essay entitled
'Critique' that the 'damaged German relationship to critique is most
comprehensible in its lack of consequence', their transformation of

critique in relation to the elusive behaviour of the thing does not seem to provide an immediate political framework for the mobilization of critique as a mode of intervention.[79] And finally, although both Benjamin and Heidegger see the need for a transformation of Kantian critique in non-transcendentalist terms and although both their projects would find common ground with the discussion of a 'critical attitude' in the Michel Foucault of 'What is Critique?', their projects are not primarily designed as archaeologically oriented tools with which to excavate a history of mentalities.[80]

What then, one might finally ask, are the ethico-political stakes of Benjamin's and Heidegger's theoretical reinscriptions of Kantian critique in terms of the thing? Is not the apparent lack of a consistent perspectival basis in their re-readings of critique evidence of a certain political lack of consequences, given that in the long and variegated history of critique, critique is typically marshalled as a form of specified resistance? Did not Marx, who famously called for a 'ruthless critique of everything that is', name his most important work on political economy a *critique*? And is not critique tied first and foremost to the political concern identified by Foucault when he lends voice to critique's 'perpetual question which would be: "how not to be governed like that, by that, in the names of those principles, with such and such an objective in mind and by means of such procedures, not like that, not for that, not by them?"'[81]

To be sure. Yet this political question, in relation to the reworkings of critique that we have encountered in Benjamin and Heidegger, is provided with a richer texture when we turn to a rather different source, Jacques Derrida. Derrida, a perspicacious and perpetual reader of both Benjamin and Heidegger, once articulated the difference between his form of deconstruction and conventional models of critique as follows:

> The *critical* idea, which I believe must never be renounced, has a history and presuppositions whose deconstructive analysis is also

necessary. In the style of the Enlightenment, of Kant, or of Marx, but also in the sense of evaluation (aesthetic or literary), *critique* supposes judgement, voluntary judgement between two terms; it attaches to the idea of *krinein* or *krisis* a certain negativity. To say that all this is deconstructible does not amount to disqualifying, negating, disavowing, or surpassing it, of doing the *critique of critique* (the way people wrote critiques of the Kantian critique as soon as it appeared), but of thinking its possibility from another border, from the genealogy of judgment, will, consciousness or activity, the binary structure, and so forth. This thinking perhaps transforms the space and, through aporias, allows the (non-positive) affirmation to appear, the one that is presupposed by every critique and every negativity.[82]

The idea of critique that emerges here both affirms critique and unsettles it, as if it were engaged in a Heideggerian *Ab-bau*, a simultaneous destruction and construction, and in a Benjaminian mode in which construction is presupposed by destruction, as the *Arcades Project* has it. While the critical idea is not to be renounced, not even by its radical transformation, it is to travel through a series of impossibilities and forms of self-resistance that open critique to its unacknowledged presuppositions.

Certainly, Derrida's project is not Benjamin's, nor is it Heidegger's. And yet, when seen from the vantage point of Derrida's reformulation of critique, Benjamin's and Heidegger's inheritance and reworking of Kantian critique in the course of their engagements with the thing assume the ethico-political urgency of a true question. To adopt this perspective is not the same as arguing that conventional political categories of left and right are displaced when they are exposed to the revolutionary thought of Benjamin and Heidegger.[83] Rather, we might say that once critique has freed itself from its origin in the primordial acts of separation and decision as well as from the metaphysics of binary thinking, its radical potentiality can begin to unfold as a non-normative dynamic, a mode of thinking and being that does not take its self-identity and self-presence, even in ethico-political terms, for granted. After all, if transformed and transformative modes of Kantian critique are still to be inherited, which is to say, are to have a future, as the heterogeneous and yet subtly imbricated projects of Benjamin and Heidegger – and, for that matter, of Derrida – suggest, this open future is to be thought and inherited as an unpredictable politics of the question. And this politics of the question, as a form of critique and its legacies, would have to begin here, with the things that surround us.

The Work of Art and Its Formal and Genealogical Determinations: Benjamin's 'Cool Place' Between Kant and Nietzsche

For Joshua Robert Gold (1971–2009)
in memoriam

Learning to inherit some of the singular and seemingly idiosyncratic ways in which Walter Benjamin himself inherits the legacies of Kant and Nietzsche in his approach to the work of art first requires another kind of inheritance. It means receiving the general legacy of the particular manner in which Benjamin's writing is replete with internal tensions and inconsistencies, a preference for apodictic statements over systematically developed deductions, and an idiosyncratic predilection for catachresis at the expense of generally accepted forms of argumentation. Self-consciously eschewing communicative transparency, his intellectual archive requires its readers and heirs to embark upon the laborious task of learning how to follow its 'own', at times strangely idiomatic, logic, and to compare his writing, not with some external standard by which it could be judged, but first and foremost *with itself*. Benjamin once referred, in a 1926 letter to Gershom Scholem, to his own self-consciously elusive and figurative mode of argumentation as an unyielding desire to think and write in a style that is 'always radical, never consistent with regard to the most important things [*immer radikal, niemals konsequent in den wichtigsten Dingen*]'.[1] Such an understanding of the critical act of thinking and writing leads him, in the material and allegorical structure of his writing, to formulate 'sentences' that, as one commentator aptly puts it, 'do not seem to be generated in the usual way; they do not entail. Each sentence is written as if it were the first, or the last.'² Benjamin's sentences stage a self-reflexive, textual model of cognition, in which language itself, rather than the formal aspects of traditional modes of argumentative presentation, becomes the agency of insight as well as of its obliteration. But this engagement with the radically textual nature of his project should not disguise the rigor and relative cohesion of Benjamin's writerly signature. For instance, as the Benjamin of *The Concept of Art Criticism in German Romanticism* puts it in relation to Nietzsche's famously fragmentary, dispersed style, 'no one will allow the fact that an author expresses himself in aphorisms as evidence against his systematic intention. Nietzsche, for instance, wrote aphoristically, even considered himself an opponent of the System, but nevertheless thought his work through in a comprehensive and unified manner according to its leading ideas and, in the end, began to write his System.'³ It is therefore no accident that Benjamin encrypts his own rigorous engagement with language itself in the first line of the epistemo-critical prologue of his study of the Baroque German mourning play, his *Trauerspiel* book as follows: 'It is the property of philosophical writing to stand, with each turn [*Wendung*], once again before the question of presentation [*vor der Frage der Darstellung zu stehen*].'⁴ This relentless and aporetic insistence on the demands of a language that resists its author and its subject matter each time it performs another *Wendung*, a turn or trope, a language that stubbornly refuses to become deceptively trans-parent, also inflects Benjamin's analyses of aesthetics and mediality. Indeed, as Samuel Weber reminds us, 'Benjamin's insistence … on the irreducible mediality of language … indicates that his concern with the "media" originates not in his later studies of radio, film and photography, but rather in his effort to elaborate a non-instrumental conception of *language*.' This conception of language, one might say, 'leads Benjamin to insist on the *irreducible immediacy of the medial*. The "medial" is "immediate" in the sense of not being instrumental.

The media must above all be distinguished from the *means*.[5] In what follows, I wish to enrich this critical inheritance of Benjamin's model of medial and aesthetic textuality by focusing on the implications of his linguistically mediated analyses of the relays between structural and historical determinations as they gain contour in his theorizations of artworks and their mediality.

In this chapter I wish to suggest, specifically, that for the Benjamin of the 1930s, whose preoccupations focus ever more relentlessly on issues of aesthetics and mediality in the broadest sense, the radical and apodictic modes of thinking and writing that are his signature could be said to coalesce around a set of issues that concern the relationship between historical – that is, genealogical – models of analysis and more strictly formal and structural ones. In fact, in our act of inheriting we could say that Benjamin's determinations of the aesthetic realm and of medium-specific problems unfold in an often overlooked bifurcation. *On one side* of this bifurcation, his ground-breaking approaches to questions of media theory and mediality (although at the time there was no such thing as 'media studies' in any formalized or institutional context), rely heavily on the genea-logical mode of argumentation that is perhaps best condensed in the programmatic conviction, expressed in the 'The Work of Art in the Age of Its Technical Reproducibility', that during *'vast historical spans of time the manner of human collectives' perception changes along with the collectives' entire mode of being-in-the-world.* The manner in which human perception organizes itself—the medium in which it takes place [*das Medium, in dem sie erfolgt*]—is conditioned not only naturally but also historically.'[6] For the mature Benjamin, the question of how to postulate the changing relationship of consciousness and perception to a work of art or a medium must not be limited to the phenomenological study of its appearance in the object world, it also must take into account the ways in which any approach to that phenomenal appearance is inflected by the historical transformations of the prevailing manner in which acts of seeing, listening, reading, thinking and even feeling are performed. The question concerning the determination of these large-scale temporal and epistemological transformations is always also one concerning the history and logic of their medial specificity.

In keeping with this view, many of Benjamin's writings on art and mediality in the 1930s fasten upon a specific aspect of their historical unfolding, propelling him to compose, among many other works, 'A Small History of Photography', 'The Rigorous Study of Art', his texts on the production and dissemination of painting and the graphic arts, as well as his meditations on such topics as film, Chaplin, Mickey Mouse, the radio, the telephone, theatre, children's books, journalism, newspapers and the publishing industry.[7] For all his interest in what could be called the medial and technological specificity of presentation, Benjamin was, as Burkhardt Lindner reminds us, 'no scholar of media studies in today's sense', and he 'did not address in any systematic way the history, technology, forms, aesthetics, or economic structures of "the media"'. This was the case in part because he belonged to a small group of early theorists whose work on technologies of writing, reproduction, the material bases of presentation, cultural memory and the socially mediated archaeologies and archives of textual and visual production first helped to found and elaborate what only decades later, during the late 1950s and 1960s, gradually came to be known and institutionally practised as media studies or, in the German context, as *Medienästhetik*.[8] It is all the more significant, then, to ask what kind of methodological stance Benjamin himself assumed in his variegated efforts to theorize aesthetics, media and the cultural and political work that technologies of presentation perform on both a structural and an historical level. More than the Hegelian model of the historical dialectic, and more than the methodological investments of such German Early Romantics as Friedrich Schlegel and Novalis, which had preoccupied him so intensely in the context of his dissertation, and perhaps even more whole-heartedly than the Marxian model of materialism and its evocations of historical determinism, Benjamin is indebted in this dimension of his mature work to the thought of Nietzsche, whose high estimation as regards the libratory potential of art and the necessity to derive an analysis of such a potential from a genealogical perspective Benjamin adapted for his own purposes.[9] While Benjamin – unlike colleagues such as Theodor W. Adorno, Ernst Bloch and Siegfried Kracauer, all of whom wrote major works on musicological questions – did not share Nietzsche's conviction, expressed in *The Birth of Tragedy*, his writings on Richard Wagner and opera, and in other central texts, that any political and philosophical analysis of the work of art and the idea of an aesthetically inflected space should proceed first and foremost through the acoustic medium of music, he did adopt Nietzsche's general methodological perspective on the genealogical derivation of concepts. In the second essay of the work that perhaps most forcefully illustrates his genealogical method, the *Genealogy of Morals*, Nietzsche famously writes that

> all concepts in which a whole process semiotically condenses itself withdraws from definition; definable is only that which has no history. [alle Begriffe, in denen sich ein ganzer Prozess semiotisch zusammen-fasst, entzieht sich der Definition; definierbar ist nur das, was keine Geschichte hat.][10]

The context of Nietzsche's definition of how concepts resist definition concerns the particular logic and execution of punishment, a concept that is intricately intertwined with the whole Western, and especially Christian, tradition of morality and its transvaluation of all values. When it comes to the major concepts that structure our history, Nietzsche argues, we are incapable of providing definitions; we can only give histories, or, in order to avoid the latent ideology of progress and teleological advancement implicit in conventional concepts of history, *genealogies*. From this Nietzschean perspective, even concepts that once did not appear to have a history – such as reason, love, the so-called human condition, a variety of emotions, the body, even common sense itself – emerge as having powerful and transformative genealogies that deserve to be analysed if one wishes to understand a concept's current valence. This is to say that the conceptual will not suffice to understand a concept; conceptual analysis, important as it is, must be enriched and supplemented by genealogical analysis, without which no major concept can be understood. There can be no regulative concept of the concept, only a conceptual history of a concept's heterogeneous mobilizations, contestations and internal struggles. In short, concepts are *inherited*.

Yet *on the other side* of Benjamin's methodological bifurcation lies the more properly formal or structural approach to a concept such as the work of art. Here, he works to delimit, on the most rigorously analytical and conceptual level, certain formal features of a mode of presentation, an experience, a felt relationship to an aesthetic constellation or of a specific way of thinking. Examples include his engagement with the structural features of the dialectical image, mourning and melancholia, the ruin, progress, allegory, messianic Now-Time and technology, among many well-known others. In this dimension of his method, Benjamin is more indebted to the formal aspects of Kantian aesthetics, especially as it is developed in the *Critique of the Power of Judgment* (1790), the attempted aesthetic mediation between the *Critique of Pure Reason*, with its emphasis on a theoretical deduction of reason as the self-critique of reason, and the *Critique of Practical Reason*, with its emphasis upon relating principles of pure reason to more experience-near questions of moral philosophy. We recall that Kant's formal aesthetic mediation pivots upon an inquiry into certain modes of deducing a priori transcendental judgements, particularly as they can be articulated in relation to the categories of the beautiful and the sublime. This inquiry proceeds by formalizing the general laws and principles according to which consciousness creates for itself the conditions and frameworks through which *Anschauung*, perception and the possibility of meaning arise even prior to any encounter between consciousness and a particular object of sense perception. In other words, Kant inquires into the conditions of possibility for any judgement and experience in the scene in which a human being exercises its faculties for judging. In the Preface to the first edition of 1790, he formulates the necessity of this particular formal inquiry as follows:

> A critique of pure reason, i.e., of our faculty for judging in accordance with a priori principles, would be incomplete if the power of judgment, which also claims to be a faculty of cognition, were not dealt with as a special part of it, even though its principles may not constitute a special part of a system of pure philosophy, between the theoretical and the practical part, but can occasionally be annexed to either of them in case of need. For if such a system, under the general name of metaphysics, is ever to come into being (the complete production of which is entirely possible and highly important for the use of reason in all respects), then the critique must previously have probed the ground for this structure down to the depth of the first foundations of the faculty of principles independent of experience, so that it should not sink in any part, which would inevitably lead to the collapse of the whole [*damit es nicht an irgend einem Teile sinke, welches des Einsturz des Ganzen unvermeidlich nach sich ziehen würde*].[11]

The 'ground' that Kant wishes to 'probe' through his formal analyses of the possibility of a priori transcendental judgements – of which one of the most central ones in the Third Critique will be the disinterested judgement 'this is beautiful' – is also shared by certain moments in Benjamin's engagements with aesthetic theory and its conditions of possibility. Although the fragmentist Benjamin, as a relentless thinker of decline and of the ruin, is, as a matter of principle, concerned to a much lesser degree than is Kant about the prospect of foundations 'sinking' away and 'the collapse of the whole', he shares with Kantian aesthetics elements of formal analysis which, even when developed in stunningly apodictic forms, will not renounce a certain allegiance to principles of fundamental deduction and a probing of the structural grounds of various conditions of possibility for cognition.

For all that separates Kant and Nietzsche in the thought of Benjamin, he does share with both of them an unfailing commitment to the cognitive specificity of a properly aesthetic experience.[12] For the Kant of the Third Critique, the realm of the aesthetic allows metaphysical thought to put *itself* into question, as it is said to be capable of providing a framework in which it becomes possible to pose questions concerning the very nature of judgement itself as well as those concerning the possibility of ascertaining a priori valid and binding judgements, even prior to consciousness having experienced an encounter with this or that phenomenon. Although it has long been suspected that Kant's concept of the aesthetic is not about actual art at all but rather merely employs the term 'art' as a placeholder for specific conditions of possibility according to which certain faculties can be described as behaving in a particular way, and even though Nietzsche distances himself from the philosophy associated with Kant – at times even ridiculing its transcendental aspirations in such central locations as Section 11 of Part One of *Beyond Good and Evil*, 'On the Prejudice of the Philosophers' – Nietzsche does share with Kant an unfailingly high estimation of the aesthetic as a phenomenon that sheds significant light on what can be known and experienced, and ultimately as a formal articulation of the thinkablity of freedom. In a well-known formulation from *The Birth of Tragedy*, Nietzsche even suggests that 'existence [*Dasein*] and the world appear justified only as an aesthetic phenomenon'.[13] From Nietzsche, Benjamin learned to think of questions of the aesthetic, in its broadest possible sense, in genealogical terms, as becomes evident, for instance, when he discusses Nietzsche in his consideration of Greek tragedy in *Origin of the German Mourning Play*, where he enlists both Nietzsche and the Blanqui of *L'éternité par les astres* for his confrontation with the idea of the eternal recurrence of the same, or when he places Nietzsche into a comparative constellation with Baudelaire in his *Central Park* fragments.[14] Indeed, according to Scholem, the young Benjamin already 'spoke a lot about the Nietzsche of the last period', mulling over the idea that 'Nietzsche was the only person in the nineteenth century, in which one only experienced "nature", to have seen historical experience.'[15] And from Kant, Benjamin inherited the belief in the necessity of the formal analysis of the aesthetic. It is no coincidence that Benjamin's initial idea for a dissertation topic was the philosophy of Kant, especially after having attended the lectures of the well-known neo-Kantian philosopher Heinrich Rickert in Freiburg and after having discussed, together with Scholem, the works on Kant by Hermann Cohen, one of the founders of the Marburg School of Neo-Kantianism.[16] Besides, there are a number of important general Kantian motifs throughout Benjamin's oeuvre that are anchored in a deep familiarity with various elements of Kant's texts, as several commentators have persuasively shown.[17]

Yet while readers of Benjamin who possess more than a rudimentary familiarity with his capacious oeuvre may have been struck, even if only on a subconscious level, by the particular bifurcation of genealogical and formal or structural determinations in his analyses, it typically remains unclear how these two modes of determination may *relate* to one another. What might be said about their relation *as relation*? From the perspective of Benjamin's unmistakable signature, what might be articulated about the ways in which they relate to each other and, by extension, about the ways in which these modes of relating inflect Benjamin's understanding of such concepts as the artwork and even the aesthetic itself? As is the case with all of his concepts and views, Benjamin does not reveal the entirety, or even the most salient features, of what he thinks about a given subject in any *single* passage, essay or book. Rather, he proceeds indirectly, non-systematically, and in a highly mediated fashion, as if to ensure that his texts perform the movements of fragmentation, dispersion and allegorical deferral of which they speak. But Benjamin does occasionally provide us with densely figurative allusions and poetically mediated figures of thought in which various elements of his speculative project shoot together in an illuminating flash to form a striking constellation. One might say that he proceeds, like his great intertext Franz Kafka, 'only allusively [*nur andeutungsweise*]' and that his manner of arguing, for all its differences from fundamental ontology, could be likened to Martin Heidegger's preference for providing, instead of systematic accounts, mere *Winke*, subtle hints or fleeting gestures pointing in a general direction. In the case of Benjamin, I wish to suggest that such instances usefully could be called 'cool places' (*kühle Stellen*), thereby mobilising the striking language that he himself employs as the designation for a key figure in the discourse of his own project. By restricting my analysis once more to one crucial passage, one *kühle Stelle*, my aim is to cast the problem into sharp relief by learning to inherit Benjamin's own methodological conviction, which pivots on 'erecting the great constructions from the smallest, sharply and cuttingly fitted building blocks' and to 'recognize in the analysis of the small singular moment the crystal of the total event [*in der Analyse des kleinen Einzelmoments den Kristall des Totalgeschehens zu erkennen*]'.[18]

In Convolut N 9a, 7 of the *Arcades Project*, we come across the following remarkable passage. We will linger with it for the remainder of this chapter:

> In every true work of art there is a place in which the one who enters it is touched by a coolness like the wind of a coming dawn. From this, it follows that art, which often has been viewed as refractory vis-à-vis any relation to progress, can serve as its genuine determination. Progress is at home not in the continuity of the course of time but in its interferences; there, where something truly New for the first time makes itself felt with the sobriety of dawn.

[In jedem wahren Kunstwerk gibt es eine Stelle, an der es den, der sich dareinversetzt, kühl wie der Wind einer kommenden Frühe anweht. Daraus ergibt sich, daß die Kunst, die man oft als refraktär gegen jede Beziehung zum Fortschritt ansah, dessen echter Bestimmung dienen kann. Fortschritt ist nicht in der Kontinuität des Zeitverlaufs sondern in seinen Interferenzen zu Hause; dort wo ein wahrhaft Neues zum ersten Mal mit der Nüchternheit der Frühe sich fühlbar macht].[19]

According to Benjamin's view, there is a place, spot or passage (*Stelle*) in a 'true' work of art that is singular and stands in counterdistinction to all the other places, spots or passages that surround it in the texture of the work. While we are not told explicitly what it is that separates a 'true' work of art from its implied opposite, a 'false' or 'untrue' work, we may surmise that the true work of art becomes re-cognizable as such precisely by virtue of the existence of such singular and radically idiomatic places. Benjamin's term 'wahr' (*in jedem wahren Kunstwerk*) should therefore be understood on at least two levels: a true work of art emerges as such when the hidden place of singularity within can be identified; and the work of art *is* something true, that is, it stands in determinable relation to what Benjamin elsewhere names its so-called truth-content, when the truth that it reveals approaches us in the form of a particular mediation. The language that here is reserved for this particular double mediation of the truth-content of a true work of art mobilizes the figure of a blowing coolness (*kühl wie der Wind anweht*). But how is it possible to recognize this place (*eine Stelle*) in the moment when one contemplates the work of art?

To suggest that there is such a *Stelle* in the artwork is to imagine the work as a form that is at odds with itself, a formal structure patterned according to certain rules and laws whose consistency is interrupted by the unexpected emergence of a radical singularity. Yet, there can be no reliable method, no formula or recipe for isolating the radical singularity of the 'cool' place that breaks with the formal aesthetic structure in which it is embedded. In what could be named its 'irruptiveness', this cool place cannot be the predictable product of merely algorhythmic or calculative reasoning. By the same token, any thoughtful identification of this place cannot be merely subjective or arbitrary either, lest it abdicate its claims to a certain truth-content and cognitive value as these emerge in the mediation of aesthetic form. In order to appreciate the cognitive value of the aesthetic experience of the work's cool place, a deliberate gesture pointing beyond the binarism of predetermination and arbitrariness would need to be thought.

At this point it may appear tempting to don the hat of the cultural historian by situating Benjamin's seemingly idiosyncratic language of *kühle Stellen*, of coolness and its relation to the aesthetic, in the cultural discourse of Weimar Germany. The Germanist Helmut Lethen's insightful history of the language and experience of coldness or coolness between the World Wars, *Verhaltenslehre der Kälte: Lebensversuche zwischen den Kriegen*, traces the various modes of coldness or coolness in their emergence as cultural determinants. Although Lethen employs the term *Kälte* rather loosely to designate a broad range of cultural phenomena without any mention of Benjamin's passage, it could be argued that this language belongs to the cultural milieu of Germany in the 1930s and 1940s. After all, why does Benjamin employ the figure of coolness or coldness to describe the wind that is blowing from the singular and unsublatable places of the true work of art? But our task here is not to make the singularity of Benjamin's language disappear into a sea of similar phenomena to which it might be compared, but rather to cast into sharp relief what may be distinctive and unsettling in his thinking of the *kühle Stelle* by comparing this thinking with *itself*.

For Benjamin, the coolness blowing toward the work's observer is felt in the moment when a rigorous and sensitive *displacement*, or change in positions, has been effected, that is, when the observer of the work has managed to gain entrance into the abyss of its internal logic and sensuo-conceptual claims. Yet what is meant by *dareinversetzen* hardly can be reduced to the humanistic gesture of proto-mimetic empathy or aesthetic identification, in which one succumbs to the double fallacy that the observer may be able, first of all, to rely on a retroactively projected artistic 'intention' which, second, may be employed to contain a work's overdeterminations and its resistance to hermeneutic disclosure – that is, to its remainderless translation into a discourse of concepts, the possibility of which would render the aesthetic experience as singularity, and therefore the existence of art itself, as obsolete. Rather, the moment of *dareinversetzen* is closer to a mad leap that lands one on the inside, a movement forward in which under-standing no longer is a standing-under, but is more akin to what in the 'Theses on the Concept of History' Benjamin terms the 'tiger's leap' (*Tigersprung*) into a different temporality of experience. The scene in which this radical moving-forward into an artwork's singular place occurs around the formal perimeters of the *Stelle* from which the coolness of a coming dawn blows.

If Benjamin employs the tropes and thought-figures of a *kühler Wind* and a *kommende Frühe* to characterize the sensuo-conceptual encounter with the true work of art, his language also points to something beyond the here-and-now presence of the singular place from which the cool breeze emerges. Just as the cool place is determined on a *structural* level by a nonself-identity that is predicated upon its difference from the places and passages that surround it, on a *temporal* level it is defined by an untimely nonself-identity that points to an elsewhere. For on the temporal level, the coolness blowing at the observer is not merely an experience of presence, it is the *Wind einer kommenden Frühe*, that is, the dawn or earliness that is yet to come, one which only can be intimated in the now-time of the aesthetic experience. Congruent with Benjamin's interest in the future-directedness even of genealogical analysis and of historical excavation, that is, parallel to his intellectual commitment to articulating, always one more time, always in different terms, the 'Program of a Coming Philosophy', as he entitles his 1919 Kant essay, the cool blowing of this aesthetic experience is one which is saturated with the possibility of futurity itself.

That this coolness of the aesthetic experience is mediated by a textual model, that is, defined by the experience of its linguistic nature (in the broadest sense of its textuality), is driven home by an intertextual relay between Benjamin's formulation and one we find in Nietzsche. In 'On Truth and Lie in an Extramoral Sense', Nietzsche articulates a theory of language that pivots upon its irreducible figurative character. Just following the essay's famous metaphor of a metaphor (in which language is defined as 'a mobile army' of metaphors and metonymies), we find a less well-known staging of the figurativity of language and truth strikingly cast in the language of coolness. Given that one of Nietzsche's main points in this essay is to assert, and then to theorize, the metaphoricity of all utterances – and even of the truth content of thought itself – this essay's own figures must be taken especially seriously, lest the presentation of the argument be taken to disregard the argument's own claims. Nietzsche writes:

> Whereas every illustrative metaphor is individual and without equal and hence always capable of eluding classification, the great construction of concepts displays the rigid regularity of a Roman columbarium and exhales in the realm of logic the rigor and coolness [*jene Strenge und Kühle*] characteristic of mathematics. Whoever is touched by this cool breath [*Wer von dieser Kühle angehaucht wird*] will hardly believe that even the concept, which is bony and eight-cornered as a die and just as transposable, remains nevertheless merely as a *residue of a metaphor*, and that the illusion inherent in the artistic translation of a nerve stimulus into images is, if not the mother, then the grandmother of every concept.[20]

Nietzsche's passage suggests that, while those metaphors that serve as an illustrative example of another point may resist the classificatory impulses of generic designation, the general structure of metaphor

itself – the metaphoricity of metaphor – emerges in the larger logic
that prevails upon all mobilizations of metaphor, regardless of their
specific function in a given context. In this larger structure, within
the metaphoricity of metaphor, the rigorous coolness breathes at
us ('*atmet ... jene Strenge und Kühle aus*'). To be breathed at by this
coolness ('*wer von dieser Kühle angehaucht wird*') may propel one to
assume that the realm of the conceptual is structured by the same
apparently logical and self-identical architecture as the mathematical
foundations of certain solid structures. But this, for Nietzsche, is
an illusion. Instead, the concept is but the residue of its metaphoric
dissimulations. The transformation of an illusion into a concept via
the uncontrollable workings of figurative language lurks in the genealogical background of any concept; it is part of its family history. This
transformative mechanism may be genealogically closer at hand (in
the form of the figure of a mother) or at a further remove (the figure
of a grandmother), but it structures every concept, even the one
that appears most self-identical, most present to itself. Nietzsche's
rhetorical mobilization of *die Kühle*, and of being '*angehaucht*' by that
Kühle when one encounters the concepts and its figurative dissimulations implicitly calls forth a stance in which this initial *Kühle* also
must be resisted in its rational, logical, Appolinian pretensions.
While *die Kühle* for Nietzsche needs to be interrogated as a form of
deception, that is, installed as the fundamental condition upon which
a far-reaching critique of language and its concepts is to be based,
Benjamin's *kühle Stelle* works to effect another kind of opening – not
one that first requires to be undone but one that itself causes a sort
of undoing, a moment of surprise and incommensurability in the
artwork that opens up the aesthetic realm to its temporal and structural determinations and even overdeterminations. While Benjamin
shares Nietzsche's figurative and textual model of the concept, his
language works dialectically to appropriate Nietzsche's in order to
brush it against the grain – that is, the figure of coolness or *Kühle* of

the *kühle Stelle* that is shared by both writers is charged in Benjamin's version with a certain revolutionary saturation within the realm of aesthetic form.

For Benjamin, the potentially revolutionary saturation of the artwork with the possibility of future experience redefines the relationship between the aesthetic and the concept of progress. If the realm of aesthetic experience once was regarded as standing in a 'refractory' relationship to progress, as Benjamin claims, then the reading that this passage offers recasts this relation in very different terms. The aesthetic form no longer is the expression of ·
a teleology of progress and its putative, triumphant improvements (in fact, Nietzsche's genealogical model already had made this view untenable), but rather makes a certain determination of the concept of progress possible. The argument that Benjamin at first sight seems to put forward is that, through a specific engagement with the *kühle Stellen*, the relationship between art and progress could be re-established according to a model of recuperation. That is to say, through the aesthetic stance (one hesitates to call it a method) that he offers, the connection between aesthetic forms and the empirical elements attached to the idea of progress, long discredited by critical thought, could be reunited. But this is not Benjamin's point. Rather, what an abiding engagement with the 'cool places' of an artwork enables is a new and actual determination (*echte Bestimmung*) of the very concept of progress. This determination need not entail a rapprochement between art and progress; on the contrary, it may well make visible the ways in which this determination, and the many determinations yet to come in the *kommende Frühe*, necessitate a dialectical reconsideration of the relation between the aesthetic and the concept (or ideology?) of progress. This dialectical reconsideration must not content itself with diagnosing a 'refractory', negative or positively supplementary relation between the realm of the aesthetic and the idea of progress. Rather, it would have to commence on the far side

of these known positions. The *echte Bestimmung* of which Benjamin speaks would break with any kind of assumed continuity in the unfolding of temporality, both as far as the artwork is concerned and in relation to progress itself. To disrupt the teleology of progress, its ideology of continuity and its horror of the spectre of regression, leads to a kind of untimeliness, something radically *Unzeitgemäßes*, as Nietzsche would put it, that, for Benjamin, names the condition of possibility for a rethinking of the relation between aesthetic experience and progress. This is why, in Benjamin's model, progress has little to do with the continuity of time and its sequential unfolding but rather inhabits or is at home (*ist zu Hause*) in its uncontainable 'interferences'.

Yet what are these interferences? How might one locate them in one's encounter with an aesthetic form and with the belief in progress? Benjamin defines these interferences, which ultimately may be coextensive with the *kühle Stellen* (although he is not explicit in this regard), as the appearance of something *wahrhaft Neues* (echoing the language of the first sentence, which speaks of the *wahre Kunstwerk*). The newness of this truly new is not a mere repetition, the mimetic return of something already known, experienced or allegedly 'represented' in the work of art as though it pre-existed that very work, but rather a newness which for the first time (*zum ersten Mal*) makes itself felt. It is worth noting that this making-itself-felt of the newness which emerges in the interferences of temporality and in the cool places of artworks is not to be thought of in terms of an elated intoxication or heightened sense of passion. Rather, this particular newness makes itself felt with a certain sobriety, a *Nüchternheit der Frühe*, a sobriety that only daybreak, the quiet and uncertain dawn of something that is still to come, can evoke. The sobriety of earliness, the *Nüchternheit der Frühe* that Benjamin casts into sharp relief is one in which consciousness awakes, not from a dream in order to be a fully self-present, transcendental, autonomous subject, but rather as if from the excesses of a Dionysian frenzy that have left their marks. It is instructive in this context to recall the language that Benjamin employs in his 1930 essay on Kracauer, where he stages the radical commitments of the latter's writings in related terms. He finds in Kracauer's work the mark of a 'rag-picker, at early dawn [*Lumpensammler frühe im Morgengrauen*], who picks up with his stick rags of speech and scraps of language in order to toss them, groaning and reluctant, a little hung over, into his cart … A rag-picker, early—at the dawn of the day of revolution.'[21] It is perhaps with a certain hangover that revolutionary consciousness opens up to the unfathomable possibilities and demands that are blowing its way from the coolness of newness itself.

The theologically inflected dimension of this model cannot be denied. Yet this is not the place for an extensive discussion of Benjamin's unorthodox messianism, nor for a reconsideration of the relation that he posits between aesthetics and a political theology (Chapter 3 has begun to make certain suggestions in that direction).[22] Benjamin's orientation here is once again close to Kafka's, who writes: 'Believing in progress does not mean believing that progress already has occurred. That would be no belief [*An Fortschritt glauben heißt nicht glauben, dass ein Fortschritt schon geschehen ist. Das wäre kein Glauben*].'[23] Benjamin, who cites this passage in his 1934 essay on Kafka, which we discussed at length in Chapter 2, shares with the writer the conviction that the belief in progress always also entails an unacknowledged residual attachment, as if through a kind of negative theology, to the belief-structure of belief itself. If the telos of progress, in the sense that postulates Enlightenment as a form of freedom from mere belief, is, among other things, the very questioning of the logic of belief, then the deferred action of progress – a progress believed either to have taken place or not to have taken place – would, in a dizzying vertigo of dialectical causality, create a mutually conditioning yet rejecting relationship between belief and progress. We cannot exclude the possibility that Benjamin, as a rigorous reader of Kafka, wishes to saturate his own reading of the aesthetic in relation to the belief in progress with this relentless dialectic.

Yet what a reading of Benjamin's passage also reveals is that its complex mobilizations of the *kühle Stelle* in the artwork enact the multiply mediated relationships between the structural and the genealogical modes of analysis in his engagement with aesthetic form. Is not the stepping forward into the cool place of the artwork, into the spot or passage that will not be contained by what surrounds it, the first step toward its formal and structural analysis? Is not the process whereby consciousness engages with the intricacies of the cool place an enactment of the formal and structural ways in which it *relates* to the work of art? And is, by the same token, the 'other' kind of temporality that opens up through that engagement with the *kühle Stelle* – an engagement in which something *wahrhaft Neues* makes itself felt and in which the continuity of temporality as well as the historical attachments of the belief in a certain kind of progress come to the fore as deeply problematic – not the expression of a genealogical way of relating to a phenomenon? While Benjamin never fully explains how the formal and the genealogical relate in his thinking, he does on occasion provide a *kühle Stelle* in which that relation is staged. As his way of thinking and arguing dictates, 'I have nothing to say. Only to show [*Ich habe nichts zu sagen. Nur zu zeigen*].'[24] What our passage about the *kühle Stelle* shows is precisely why its 'showing' – as opposed to merely saying, a saying that would ignore the logic and requirements of its own strategic operations – in the full Benjaminian sense is necessary. It also suggests why in Benjamin's work on aesthetics and, by extension, the medial specificity of cognition and experience, the formal-structural and the genealogical dimension of analysis and argumentation are dialectically intertwined and, indeed, mutually saturated with the open-ended interpretative possibilities and unfathomable demands of the other.

Finally, in our attempts at inheriting Benjamin's uneasy legacy and its potentialties we would do well to recall that Benjamin always wishes to understand his meditations on the aesthetic and its media as properly *political* acts, even in those instances in which the political stakes of these meditations are not obvious. The most explicit formulation of this political concern inscribed in his illuminations of art and media is to be found in the famous preface to the Artwork essay. There, Benjamin insists that 'outmoded concepts' such as 'creativity and genius, eternal value and mystery' encourage 'a processing of data in the fascist sense', and that what he wishes to accomplish with his philosophical investigations of art and media is the development of concepts that 'differ from the more familiar terms in that they are completely useless for the purposes of fascism'.[25] What Benjamin ultimately works to think in his theory of the aesthetic and of its medial networks is the way in which the political is always mobilized as an act of presentation, language, mediation and ceaseless – at times even aporetic – interpretation.[26] From this perspective, the *kühle Stelle* also could be read as the name for a locus of political reflection as it is mediated by questions raised by the experience of aesthetic and medial-specific presentation. In that sense, Benjamin's reflections on the *kühle Stelle* could help to shed light on some of our contemporary attempts to rethink the relays among the aesthetic, the medial and the political under the conditions not of 1930s Fascism, but of global Empire. For instance, the idea of a *kühle Stelle* could be made to resonate with Alain Badiou's recent theses on contemporary art, in which he suggests that it 'is better to do nothing than to contribute to the invention of formal ways of rendering visible that which Empire already recognizes as existent'.[27] For Badiou, today's 'art can only be made from the starting point of that which, as far as Empire is concerned, does not exist. Through its abstraction, art renders this in-existence visible. This is what governs the formal principle of every art: the effort to render visible … that which, for Empire (and so by extension for everyone, though from a different point of view), does not exist.[28] A certain relation to Benjamin's project becomes visible here. What is always also embedded in the work's *kühle Stelle* is, after all, a certain abstraction that works to render visible what is not known by the dominant way (or prescription) of looking to exist as such. The *kühle Stelle*, itself a kind of gap, lack or fissure, opens onto ways of seeing that are saturated by the unpredictable and therefore non-instrumentalizable qualities of a ceaseless philosophical and political recalibration. This is one of the variegated iterations, always modulated with different conceptual accents, of what Benjamin calls his 'formulation of revolutionary demands in the politics of art'.[29] One way of inheriting the *kühle Stelle* is, we might say, the insight that it embodies, of necessity, one of the modes of presentation in non-imperial art.

Much like Nietzsche's famous figure of language as a well-worn coin whose stamp is no longer visible – the metaphor of a metaphor that is lodged at the core of 'On Truth and Lie in an Extramoral Sense' – Benjamin's *kühle Stelle* vis-à-vis the artwork's *kühle Stelle* is itself the secret *kühle Stelle* within the fragmented, ruinous, unwieldy and unlikely work of art that we call the *Arcades Project*. (Benjamin betrays his awareness of the aesthetic status of this work when he refers to its 'inadmissibly "poetic"' character.[30]) The *kühle Stelle* ultimately functions as both an instantiation and as the legacy of Benjamin's multiply determined engagements with the aesthetic realm of medium-specific cognition, an epigrammatic enactment of the larger relation that he puts to work – '*immer radikal, niemals consequent*' – in his idiosyncratic discourses on method. The language of the *kühle Stelle*, situated between the legacies of Kant and Nietzsche, emanates from the constellation of images and figures that bear the mark of methodological urgency. 'The read image', Benjamin reminds us, 'that is, the image of the Now of recognizability, bears to the highest degree the stamp of that critical, dangerous moment that lies at the ground of all reading.'[31] Pretty *cool*.

Going with Time: A Miniature on Time and Photography after Benjamin[1]

'History breaks down into images, not into stories.'

Walter Benjamin

Two sentences to begin with, two figures of thought to be inherited, two enigmatic axioms to which we will return again and again, and which, for their part, will haunt us as an uneasy legacy in many different ways: Photography goes with time. Photography will have gone with time. What can that mean? The German expression 'mit der Zeit gehen', going with time or going with the times, is inscribed in an elegant and at once unruly dispersal of meaning that is worthwhile to recollect. To go with time first of all means to involve oneself in new developments, a supposed advance, a new behavioural pattern, a changing opinion formation, but also to conform to a currently prevailing fashion. The person who goes with time considers himself to be up to date, is relevant to the times, does not engage in untimely observations, does not withhold his approval but rather joins in, affirms whatever presently exists – perhaps even up to the point at which he, as one says in German, 'blesses time [*das Zeitliche segnen*]', that is, passes on. In this sense, he goes *with* time and not perchance *without* it or *against* it; he does not go empty-handed, but rather allows himself to be taken by the hand by time, to follow it, to obey it. Wherever he may go when he goes *with* time, he goes along with it; he is its companion and follower. To go with the times, however, requires not only going *with* the times, but rather precisely going with *the* times, which always means with *these* particular times and no other. At the same time, there also is the resonance of a countervailing idea in the *the* of the going-with-the-times, suggesting that what is meant by the times is not only this or that particular time, this or that point in time, but rather time as such, time as time. To go with time then always also would mean to open oneself up to the temporality of time, actively to submit to it and to recognize it as a co-ordinate of existence. Finally, the verb 'to go' also ought to give us cause for reflection on the idea of someone or something having *gone* with time. This ambulatory element of going-with-the-times enters into linguistic awareness when one considers not only that the dynamic motion of going re-enacts the movement of time, but also that the verb 'to go' calls forth something fundamentally active and mobile that tightly imbricates the being of human action with the experience of temporality. The German language, in particular, may have knowledge of this imbrication, because, in a remarkable and peculiar way, it holds in stock for the word 'verb' – which derives from the Latin *verbum* – the designation *Tätigkeitswort*, 'action word', *as well as* the designation *Zeitwort*, 'time word'. The concurrent differentiatedness and simultaneity of a verb's activity and temporality here manifest themselves in an especially striking way, endowing the 'going' in 'going-with-the-times' with its singular force and vividness.

By the same token, going-with-the-times always also attests to a certain mortality, a fundamental orientation toward its own finitude. With time – that is, more or less slowly, gradually and with increasing measure, possibly in a measured transition [*Über-gang*] from a going or *gait* [*Gang*] to the constantly accelerating *course* [*Lauf*] of time – we are going, stepping down, disappearing, taking leave, passing away. The German idiom *Kommt Zeit, kommt Rat* tells us alternatively that in time counsel will be offered and that time itself will offer counsel; yet, as time comes, so comes departing. For going with time also means aging, a process that Goethe, for good reason, once defined as a 'gradual receding [*Rücktritt*] from appearance', that is, a sort of stepping-back or stepping-down from a self and what exists within and around it.[2] One goes with time when it is time to go, high time; with time one becomes the person who must go, the going one who actually already from birth onward approaches his future going, the parting, the last walk [*der letzte Gang*].

In what sense, then, can we suggest that photography goes with time and that in the end it always will have gone with time? This suggestion cannot mean merely that, in a material sense, a print or exemplar of a photograph grows pale with time and with exposure to certain effects of light, even if that is the case and time does make itself irrefutably felt with the fading of an image. The suggestion also cannot be meant only in the technological sense, whereby photography as a technical medium adapts itself to time and its newest possibilities, although such adaptation undoubtedly takes place. Photo-graphy – that is, writing with light – certainly goes with time when it develops from its middle-of-the-nineteenth-century origins in early forms such as the daguerreotype through the analog process of negative-based photography invented by William Henry Fox Talbot, up to the digital photography that today, in the second decade of the twenty-first century, is so omnipresent that it is already built into so-called smartphones and similarly easily portable devices of daily communication and network linkage. The going-with-time of photography is always also a history of photographic technology, even the history of technology itself. But what is of concern here is much more than the technological going-with-time that always is oriented toward an already predetermined perspective on supposed progress and its marketability. At stake, rather, is a more originary going-with-time, one whose essence cannot be reduced to the technical, to what is technologically achievable, or to a form of empirical problem solving. On the contrary, it concerns a going-with-time that allows the relation between human experience and its photographically mediated reflection to enter into consciousness.

Especially through photographs that mean something to us, that address us, that are intimate to us for the most varied reasons, the experience of going-with-time speaks, even when it may not be the intended or manifest subject of a particular image. A photograph first of all interrupts the passage or gait of time, working to capture something that threatens to disappear forever; every photograph also demarcates an historical archive, staging a technically mediated interruption of time that subsequently allows an image to be brought back as often as desired, made visible and exhibited anew. Yet what found itself in front of the shutter of the apparatus in the moment in which the release button was pressed has become history immediately upon its recording; it no longer exists in its recorded condition, already having become something different through the dynamic influence of time and space. We have this experience in particular when we observe a portrait of ourselves that was taken many years ago and shows us as a younger, different, almost foreign-seeming person, or when we observe a photographic portrait of another who already has gone so far with time that he is dead. Fundamentally, however, this process of becoming different, and its attendant estrangement and historicization, commence immediately after the picture is taken. When I observe my just-taken portrait, already I am no longer the person that I was only a moment ago; I have changed, even if only imperceptibly, and therefore already have begun the process of transformation that, in the course of the subsequent days, weeks, months, years or even decades, will separate me ever more noticeably from the moment of this recording, and, in this way, will move me ever closer to the experience of finitude.

Every photograph, in so far as it goes with time and, in turn, allows what it depicts to go with time, is a small historical triumph that has wrested a memento from the passage or gait of time and, at the same time, a place of mourning and of melancholy for the imminent or already experienced leave-taking. A photograph, regardless of how cheerful the subject matter that it depicts may be, always also carries grief, as though it were a little gravestone. And when one who still lives contemplates a photograph that depicts himself, he is dealing with a sort of estate while still alive, one which, in the realm of the image, will outlive him and sooner or later entirely take his place, that is, will come to 'represent' him in more than one way. If a photograph in which we are depicted is circulated among our friends, we may overhear how they converse about our picture; in this way, we make present to ourselves the function that our picture comes to serve, such that the experience borders on the uncanny because here we symbolically are attending our own anticipated funeral, as if we were dead and yet still found ourselves among the living. This photographically mediated experience is perhaps comparable to the uncanny moment in Edgar Allan Poe's story 'The Facts in the Case of M. Valdemar' in which M. Valdemar, on his deathbed after his demise, continues to speak by way of providing commentary on his own condition: 'and now—now—*I am dead*.'[3]

Photography goes with time; in its passage or gait, it takes us by the hand, allowing us, even exhorting us, to reflect upon and to speak about the experience of this going or this going-along. One might say that the photograph of a deceased person in particular – possibly someone with whom we were acquainted, that is, a person who possesses a proper name in a particular idiomatic form in relation to us – enjoins us to reflect upon the meaning of photography as a technologically mediated memento mori. In his meditations on photography, Roland Barthes makes reference to an 1865 image by Alexander Gardner showing a young man named Lewis Payne in handcuffs shortly before his execution for an assassination attempt. 'The photograph is handsome, as is the boy', we read there. Barthes adds: '*He is going to die*. I read at the same time: *This will be* and *this has been*.'[4] In so far as it can be asserted that the young man is dead and he will die, the photograph here goes with time – that is, along with time, extending its hand two times to time, namely, each time the other one. On the one hand, the beautiful lad already has been dead for countless years, belonging to another century in which he went with time in his own way, particular to him; on the other hand, the photograph also arrests a moment in which the represented person is still alive, albeit conscious of being consecrated to death. While contemplating this image, as well as the one of his mother that is not reproduced in his text, Barthes has the following experience: 'I observe with horror an anterior future of which death is the stake. By giving me the absolute past of the pose ... the photograph tells me death in the future. What *pricks* me is the discovery of this equivalence.' He continues: 'In front of the photograph of my mother as a child, I tell myself: she is going to die; I shudder like Winnicott's psychotic patient, *over a catastrophe which has already occurred.* Whether or not the subject is already dead, every photograph is this catastrophe.'[5] Even if a photograph does not depict someone who has been sentenced to death, the double gesture of the already-long-since and the not-yet remains inscribed in every photograph, because 'each photograph always contains this imperious sign of my future death ... however attached it seems to be to the excited world of the living'.[6] If every photograph can be regarded as a catastrophe that already has come to pass, then a moment of horror, of discord, and of unfinished mourning repeats itself in the medium of the recorded image. What once stood long enough before the camera and was struck by sufficient light (*photos*) to make its inscription (*graphein*) possible, functions, simultaneously, as a witness to a former reference and to its suspension in the time with which the photograph (the *Lichtbild* or light-picture, as the earliest photograph tellingly was called in German) goes. What is interrupted here is the idea of a continuity of temporality in which what is photographed as well as what once existed (the historical reference) stages what is present (something that under certain circumstances stands before a camera) also as what is yet to come (in the future of the catastrophe which is still to be repeated.)

If Barthes speaks of a childhood photograph of his already deceased mother as testimony of a death that is yet to come and that long since already has occurred, as a catastrophe that is yet to be experienced and at the same time no longer exists, he also implicitly evokes the special status that a childhood photograph of a dead person in particular occupies. To be sure, the childhood photograph of a deceased person is related to all other photographs, is subject to the general 'laws' of photography, and therefore undoubtedly is like all other photographs or light-pictures. Because of its particular character, however, the childhood photograph nevertheless occupies a separate position, denotes a singular genre, refers with an unmistakable gesture and even embodies something like a unique signature in the act of writing with light.

In his notes published in the *Jüdische Rundschau* on the occasion of the tenth anniversary of Kafka's death in 1934, Walter Benjamin describes a photograph of the writer under the title 'A Childhood Photograph' as follows: 'There is a childhood photograph of Kafka; seldom has a "poor, brief childhood" become image in a more touching way.'[7] The photograph from Kafka's youth shows him oddly clothed and with a melancholic gaze in a studio outfitted with a variety of easels and drapery as was customary for a photographer's atelier in the nineteenth century (Figure 1).

The phrase 'poor, brief childhood' that Benjamin suggests coalesces, in this portrait, into an image originates from a passage in Kafka's volume *A Hunger Artist* published in 1924. In the story 'Josephine, the Singer or The Mouse People' we encounter the following language: 'Something of our poor, brief childhood is in it; something of lost, irretrievable happiness.'[8] Does the photographic image, particularly that of a child – apart from the depicted moment of *this* appearance before the recording device and this historical and time-interrupting inscription in presentation – not always also capture the temporality of what is finite, made visible by the image

Fig. 1: Franz Kafka, Childhood photograph (Courtesy of Walter Benjamin Archiv, Akademie der Künste, Berlin).

of a person as a product of the camera, as above all else one that accompanies brevity and fleetingness? As a technologically mediated memento mori, the childhood photograph always also enacts the gradually emerging simultaneity of a non-foreclosed beginning and its preliminary closure in the realm of the image; here, the photograph is both a birth certificate and a gravestone. The childhood photograph goes with time.

Let us consider a childhood photograph that was taken in Germany around 1937, in other words, shortly after the appearance of Benjamin's reflections on Kafka's childhood photograph (Figure 2).

Fig. 2: Photograph of a child, Germany, c. 1937. (Author's archive)

We are looking not at an arbitrary childhood photograph but rather at one that speaks to us, one that for inexplicable reasons draws our gaze to itself, and one that demands to be studied again and again without at first glance seeming to be anything other than an ordinary photograph. 'A picture', as Wittgenstein tells us for good reason, 'held us captive. And we could not get outside it, for it lay in our language, and language seemed only to repeat it to us inexorably.'[9] We see a boy who appears to be blonde with dark, clear eyes, about two years of age. He is dressed in a sort of gender-neutral bodice, as was perhaps not uncommon in rural children's fashion of that time; beneath, a shirt is visible as well as a short pair of pants in a lighter shade; underneath that, a darker pair of leggings. Along with these, he is wearing half-height children's shoes, possibly made of brown leather. He is standing in front of a tree that, for its part, is located behind a wire fence. It is as though this fence marked a boundary between the boy and the tree, from which a sort of chain appears to hang down, that at the same time separates and connects. Carrying a small stick or little toy in his right hand in a mildly absentminded way and with an almost tender persuasion and trust in God, the child is looking to his right, in other words, away from the camera, which is positioned slightly to the boy's left, whereas his feet are pointing somewhat more in the direction of the person taking the picture. Who is taking the picture? Is the gaze that is directed to the boy's right his spontaneous reaction to a call from that side? And who is standing there? Although the invisible presence of the photographer is confirmed only by the existence of the picture, the presence of an additional person is suggested by a shadow that appears in the lower third of the photograph on the left and runs parallel to the shadow that the boy himself casts. Is there a relationship between the boy and this person who only is visible to the observer by allusion? How, in photography, does what is imaged relate to what is not imaged, or to what only is partially imaged, that is, to what is obliquely suggested? Does the boy's facial expression convey curiosity, surprise, hopefulness or even – below the slightly lowered eyebrows that are reminiscent of little Kafka's – nascent concern? How does the 'poor, brief childhood' become image here? What is the status in this light-picture of 'the lost, irretrievable happiness' of which Kafka knows? Does the imaged child not patiently preside here before a lens and an existence that both wish to be focused?

To say, as Barthes does with regard to the childhood photograph of his mother, that the young person who is depicted is not only dead but is also yet to die, means that the photograph will have gone with time. The grammatical tense of the 'will have gone' is the future perfect, that is, the time which, although observed from the standpoint of the grammatical present, has not yet taken place, but already is arrested as something that at some point in the future will have been completed and already permits an anticipatory reference back in time. For in the photograph of the child, death resides twice over, as announced and as deferred. Photography will have gone with time, hand-in-hand with finitude itself.

In the charged relation between announcement and deferral, the photograph of the boy raises further questions that historically and intellectually are so far-ranging that only a few of them – and only in a telegraphic manner – can be captured through its contemplation. How will the boy who, like his photograph, will have gone with time, survive – if at all – the terror and the suffering that Nazi fascism is already kindling and will soon multiply? What will become of his parents and family during the war years? Will the one who took the photo and that other person whose shadow also attends the photographic scene survive all that has already occurred or is imminent, that is, dictatorship, the rule of terror, world war, genocide, mass murder, displacement and expulsion? Will time hold a protective hand over the boy or abandon him to his fate? Will the boy who goes with time be orphaned, killed or saved? Will his future trauma, as the wound is called in Greek, change him into another human being? Will he, during and after his trauma, still be able to remember both the pre-traumatic scene of this photograph and the self that is still in a position to devote its more or less un-wounded attention to play, merriment and freedom? Will he ever again be able to see the tree before which he stands, or will he, with time, experience not only the transcendental homelessness of which Lukács speaks but also his own? Will he perhaps live as a nomad or be taken in as a refugee elsewhere? Which memory images of the boy's 'poor, brief childhood' will have left an indelible mark on him? Will the imaged child himself at some point photograph children who are going with time?

In his 1927 reflections on photography, Siegfried Kracauer writes: 'The meaning of memory images is linked to their truth content … The last image of a person is that person's actual *history*. This history omits all characteristics and determinations that do not relate in a significant sense to the truth intended by a liberated consciousness.'[10] He adds: 'How a person represents this history does not depend purely on his or her natural constitution or on the pseudo-coherence of his or her individuality; thus, only fragments of these assets are included in his or her history … In a photograph, a person's history is buried as if under a layer of snow.'[11] What can be seen of a person in a photograph only ever can offer a partial perspective on his history and his existence, even when the person, like the child who is imaged here, is depicted in full height. The photograph is a fragment of what can be meant by a historicity made visible; it participates in the truth to whose content it must be medially attached, yet for which it still cannot *stand-in* according to the terms of presentation. The memory images enter consciousness as fragments, but they cannot be assembled there into a totality of experience or of meaning. By the same token, photographs do not act merely as reproductions of something that already exists, and that also would have existed without them, since without the mnemotechnics of the image and its omnipresence there would be hardly any space for memory images at all. This is so even if the history of a person can never be observed and interpreted directly, but rather lies buried beneath a blanket of snow which one approaches not with a kind of hermeneutic snow plough but instead with the patient art of explication that is practised by a reader of traces, one who tracks the traces of time that are always marked in an unexpected way and who, in the truest sense of the word, goes with time.

In the process of describing what is most likely an imaginary scene, in which descendants contemplate an old photograph of their grandmother that shows the lady as a young woman in her early twenties, Kracauer imagines the grandchildren looking on with amusement at the fashion that is worn in the picture, a style that has long since been replaced by a series of completely different fashions. Their state of amusement, however, is suffused with a ghostly premonition: 'They laugh, and at the same time they shudder. For through the ornamentation of the costume from which the grandmother has disappeared, they think they glimpse a moment of time past, a time that passes without return.'[12] 'Although', the passage proceeds, 'time is not photographed like the smile or the chignon, the photograph itself, so it seems to them, is a representation of time. Were it the photograph alone that endowed them with duration, they would not at all outlast mere time; rather, time would create images for itself out of them.'[13] There can be no fashion that does not go with time; that which is fashionable is always also a going-with-the-times, a wanting-to-be-on-top-of-the-times, a mode of being for which standstill represents an impossibility and that gives itself over with a more or less affirmative enthusiasm to the arbitrariness of whatever is currently new.[14] As that which goes with the times, photography itself might create the impression of representing a fashion that is in the process of perpetual transformation; perhaps this is, in fact, the unspoken assumption that the grandchildren, amused by the unfashionable fashion of their photographed grandmother, hold. What would be much more disconcerting, however, is the notion that things are, in a certain sense, the other way around: that time, for its part, creates images for itself out of human subjects, pictures in which existence – together with the consciousness that reflects upon it – is staged as the name of an experience that is directed toward its own finitude, indeed, toward finitude as such.

Viewed from this perspective, time acts as a sort of diligent collector who zealously pastes photographs of the deceased, or those who will die in the future, into its imaginary album. In the death-oriented medium of photography, time will have gone *with itself*. Does not time, when it goes with itself, always also turn the pencil of nature, as Talbot referred to photography in the middle of the nineteenth century, into the pencil of finitude and death? For photography, as the proper inheritor of time itself, goes with time, and it will have gone with time.

Notes

Chapter One

1 Georg Wilhelm Friedrich Hegel, *Differenz des Fichteschen und Schellingschen Systems der Philosophie. Werke. Vol 2: Jenaer Schriften 1801–1807*, eds. Eva Moldenhauer and Karl Markus Michel (Frankfurt am Main: Suhrkamp, 1986), 17.

  When not otherwise indicated, translations in this book are my own. When published translations are cited, I have occasionally modified them in order either to enhance their fidelity to the original or to emphasize a certain aspect or tone of a given phrase or passage that is fully present in the original but may be less graspable in an existing translation. *What* Benjamin says can never be separated from *how* he says it.

2 Walter Benjamin, 'La Traduction—Le pour et le contre', *Gesammelte Schriften*, eds. Rolf Tiedemann and Hermann Schweppenhäuser (Frankfurt am Main: Suhrkamp, 1991), vol. 6, 157–8, here 158; 'Translation—For and Against', trans. Edmund Jephcott, *Selected Writings*, eds. Michael W. Jennings et al. (Cambridge, MA: Harvard University Press, 2002), vol. 3: 1935–8, 249–52, here 249.

3 Howard Eiland and Michael W. Jennings, *Walter Benjamin: A Critical Life* (Cambridge, MA: Harvard University Press, 2014), 3.

4 An analysis of Benjamin's radio talks for children is offered by Jeffrey Mehlman, *Walter Benjamin for Children: An Essay on His Radio Years* (Chicago: University of Chicago Press, 1993). For a penetrating recent reading of Benjamin's scribbles during his drug protocols, see Thomas Schestag, '"Diese Hand [. . .]": Walter Benjamin kritzelt', *Lesen – Sprechen – Schreiben (Kritzeln)* (Berlin: Matthes und Seitz, 2014), 67–117.

5 Norbert Bolz, 'Gnosis and Systems Theory: A Conversation between Norbert Bolz and Michael Hirsch', trans. Steven Lindberg, in *Adorno: The Possibility of the Impossible*, eds. Nicolaus Schafhausen, Vanessa

Joan Müller and Michael Hirsch (Berlin: Lukas & Sternberg, 2003), 93–110, here 105.

It should be noted here that, in counterdistinction to Bolz's position, recent years also have seen an array of especially vigorous attempts at inheriting Benjamin in previously unexpected or underdeveloped ways. See, among others, Peter Fenves, *The Messianic Reduction: Walter Benjamin and the Shape of Time* (Stanford: Stanford University Press, 2011) as well as Eli Friedlander, *Walter Benjamin: A Philosophical Portrait* (Cambridge, MA: Harvard University Press, 2012), which, each in their own way, work to situate Benjamin's work in the context of their philosophical contemporaries and the European philosophical legacy. Andrew Benjamin, *Working with Walter Benjamin: Recovering a Political Philosophy* (Edinburgh: Edinburgh University Press, 2013), Bettine Menke, *Das Trauerspiel-Buch: Der Souverän – das Trauerspiel – Konstellationen – Ruinen* (Bielefeld: Transcript, 2010) and Jan Urbich, *Darstellung bei Walter Benjamin: Die 'Erkenntniskritische Vorrede' im Kontext ästhetischer Darstellungstheorien der Moderne* (Berlin: De Gruyter, 2012) each in their own way attempt to set forth a set of principles that would help critical discourse to open to the legacy of Benjamin today – precisely by *working with* his concepts.

6   Slavoj Žižek, *First as Tragedy, Then as Farce* (London: Verso, 2009), 6.
7   Walter Benjamin, 'Trauerspiel und Tragödie', *Gesammelte Schriften*, vol. 2, 134; 'Trauerspiel and Tragedy', *Selected Writings*, vol. 1, 55.
8   Walter Benjamin, *Gesammelte Briefe*, vol. 1: 1910–18, eds. Christoph Gödde and Henri Lonitz (Frankfurt am Main: Suhrkamp, 1995), 382; *The Correspondence of Walter Benjamin*, trans. Manfred R. Jacobson and Evelyn M. Jacobson (Chicago: University of Chicago Press, 1994), 94.
9   Friedrich Nietzsche, *Also sprach Zarathustra. Kritische Studienausgabe*, vol. 4, eds. Giorgio Colli and Mazzino Montinari (Munich and Berlin: Deutscher Taschenbuch Verlag and De Gruyter, 1999), 100; *Thus Spoke Zarathustra*, trans. Adrian Del Caro, eds. Adrian Del Caro and Robert Pippin (Cambridge: Cambridge University Press, 2006), 58. This paragraph and the following one are condensed versions of my discussion of Nietzsche and Derrida in *Verwaiste Hinterlassenschaft. Formen gespentischen Erbens* (Berlin: Matthes & Seitz, 2016).

10 Nietzsche, *Also sprach Zarathustra*, 94; *Thus Spoke Zarathustra*, 54.

11 Jacques Derrida, *Spectres de Marx: L'État de la dette, le travail du deuil et la nouvelle Internationale* (Paris: Galilée, 1993), 95; *Specters of Marx: The State of the Debt, the Work of Mourning, and the New International*, trans. Peggy Kamuf (New York: Routledge, 1994), 55.

12 *Spectres de Marx*, 46; *Specters of Marx*, 21.

13 *Spectres de Marx*, 40; *Specters of Marx*, 16.

14 Stéphane Mosès, *The Angel of History: Rosenzweig, Benjamin, Scholem*, trans. Barbara Harshav (Stanford: Stanford University Press, 2009), 125.

15 For a detailed development of this argument, see Gerhard Richter, 'Can Anything Be Rescued by Defending It? Benjamin with Adorno', *differences* 21 (3) (2010): 34–52.

16 Walter Benjamin, *Passagen-Werk*, *Gesammelte Schriften*, vol. 5, 591; *The Arcades Project*, trans. Howard Eiland and Kevin McLaughlin (Cambridge, MA: Harvard University Press, 1999), 473.

17 Stanley Cavell, 'Remains to be Seen', in *Walter Benjamin and the Arcades Project*, ed. Beatrice Hanssen (London: Continuum, 2006), 259–63, here 263.

18 Walter Benjamin, *Passagen-Werk*, *Gesammelte Schriften*, vol. 5, 578; *Arcades Project*, 463.

19 Cornelius' report is cited in Burkhardt Lindner, 'Habilitationsakte Benjamin. Über ein "akademisches Trauerspiel" und über ein Vorkapitel der "'Frankfurter Schule" (Horkheimer, Adorno)', in *Walter Benjamin im Kontext*, 2nd edn, ed. Burkhardt Lindner (Königstein/Ts: Athenäum, 1985), 324–41, here 332. Lindner's essay also includes a variety of further documentary material on the political, institutional and philosophical circumstances of Benjamin's attempted *Habilitation*.

20 Ibid., 333.

Chapter Two

1 For a discussion of these and closely related figures in Benjamin, see Gerhard Richter, *Afterness: Figures of Following in Modern Thought*

and Aesthetics (New York: Columbia University Press, 2011), esp. 2–7. On Benjamin's concept of *Überleben* (survival or living on) as a textual question of citation, see Werner Hamacher, 'Intensive Sprachen', in *Übersetzen: Walter Benjamin*, ed. Christian L. Hart Nibbrig (Frankfurt am Main: Suhrkamp, 2001), 174–235. More recently, cf. Daniel Weidner, 'Fort-, Über-, Nachleben. Zu einer Denkfigur bei Benjamin', *Benjamin-Studien* 2 (2011): 161–78.

2 Walter Benjamin, 'Eduard Fuchs, der Sammler und Historiker', *Gesammelte Schriften*, vol. 2, 465–85, here 473; 'Eduard Fuchs, Collector and Historian', *Selected Writings*, vol. 3, 260–302, here 265.

3 This perspective on Benjamin's Fuchs essay is developed in Stefan Willer, '"Nachleben des Verstandenen": Walter Benjamin und das Erbe des historischen Materialismus', *Text und Kritik* 31/32 (2009): 88–96.

4 Sigrid Weigel provides a concise philological overview of the various elements of what might be called Benjamin's 'Kafka dossier', of which the 1934 essay is a central part: 'Zu Franz Kafka', in *Benjamin-Handbuch. Leben—Werk—Wirkung*, ed. Burkhardt Lindner (Stuttgart: Metzler, 2006), 543–57. Many of Benjamin's texts on Kafka, along with various notes and portions of relevant letters from the correspondence with Scholem, Adorno and Kraft are accessibly collected in Walter Benjamin, *Über Franz Kafka. Texte, Briefzeugnisse, Aufzeichnungen*, ed. Hermann Schweppenhäuser (Frankfurt am Main: Suhrkamp, 1981).

5 See Siegfried Kracauer, 'Franz Kafka', *Das Ornament der Masse* (Frankfurt am Main: Suhrkamp, 1977), 256–268; 'Franz Kafka', *The Mass Ornament: Weimar Essays*, trans. Thomas Y. Levin (Cambridge, MA: Harvard University Press, 1995), 267–278; and Theodor W. Adorno, 'Aufzeichnungen zu Kafka', *Gesammelte Schriften*, ed. Rolf Tiedemann (Frankfurt am Main: Suhrkamp, 1997), vol. 11, 243–271; 'Notes on Kafka', *Prisms*, trans. Samuel and Shierry Weber (Cambridge, MA: MIT Press, 1981), 243–271.

6 Michael W. Jennings, '"Eine gewaltige Erschütterung des Tradierten": Walter Benjamin's Political Recuperation of Franz Kafka', in *Fictions of Culture: Essays in Honor of Walter H. Sokel*, ed. Steven Taubeneck (New York: Lang, 1991), 199–214. If Benjamin's Kafka essay marks a moment of transition in his own work, it relates in turn to the

trajectory of Kafka exegesis by coaxing into being ever-renewed readings and rigorous reinterpretations. As Henry Sussman observes in an early reading, 'Benjamin's study heralds further readings of Kafka because it is built into the very clefts which Kafka's "reason and cunning have inserted" into myths.' 'The Herald: A Reading of Walter Benjamin's Kafka Study', *Diacritics* 7 (1) (1977); 42–54, here 54. Finally, for a sustained consideration of the problems that a reading of Benjamin's Kafka raises in the larger literary and philosophical context of the essay form, see Sven Kramer, *Rätselfragen und wolkige Stellen: Zu Benjamins Kafka-Essay* (Lüneburg: zu Klampen, 1991).

7 For a representative example of these tendencies, see Beda Allemann, 'Fragen an die judaistische Kafka-Deutung am Beispiel Benjamins', in *Franz Kafka und das Judentum*, eds. Karl Erich Grözinger, Stéphane Mosès and Hans Dieter Zimmermann (Frankfurt am Main: Jüdischer Verlag bei Athenäum, 1987), 35–70. A more recent assessment of Benjamin's relation to the Judaic traditions through recourse to his reading of Kafka is offered by Daniel Weidner, 'Jüdisches Gedächtnis, mystische Tradition und moderne Literatur. Walter Benjamin und Gershom Scholem deuten Kafka', *Weimarer Beiträge* 46 (2) (2002): 234–49.

8 Robert Alter, *Necessary Angels: Tradition and Modernity in Kafka, Benjamin, and Scholem* (Cambridge, MA: Harvard University Press, 1991), 22f.

9 Ibid., 80.

10 Walter Benjamin, 'Franz Kafka. Zur zehnten Wiederkehr seines Todestages', *Gesammelte Schriften*, vol. 2: 409–38, here 412. I thank my friend David Farrell Krell for our stimulating conversations about this and other passages and texts in the context of a graduate seminar we co-taught at Brown on the question of inheritance in modernity.

11 Walter Benjamin, 'Franz Kafka: On the Tenth Anniversary of His Death', *Selected Writings*, eds. Michael W. Jennings, Howard Eiland and Gary Smith (Cambridge, MA: Harvard University Press, 1999), vol. 2, 794–818, here 796.

12 One might even suggest that part of this proprietorial fluctuation also

participates in the structure of crisis and deconstitution that Avital Ronell has thoughtfully excavated from Kafka's letter in relation to the category of authority. *Loser Sons: Politics and Authority* (Urbana: University of Illinois Press, 2012), 106–51.

13 Franz Kafka, *Tagebücher. Kritische Ausgabe*, eds. Hans-Gerd Koch, Michael Müller and Malcolm Pasley (Frankfurt am Main: Fischer, 2002), 857.

14 I thank my colleague at Brown, the political philosopher Bonnie Honig, for reminding me, following the presentation of this chapter as a public lecture, of this homophonic relation.

15 Walter Benjamin, '*Über Sprache überhaupt und über die Sprache des Menschen*', *Gesammelte Schriften*, vol. 2, 140–57, here 153; 'On Language as Such and on the Language of Man', *Selected Writings*, vol. 1, 62–74, here 71.

16 Walter Benjamin, *Gesammelte Briefe*, vol. 6, 1938–40, eds. Christoph Gödde and Henri Lonitz (Frankfurt am Main: Suhrkamp, 2000), 105–15, here 112f.; *The Correspondence of Walter Benjamin and Gershom Scholem, 1932–1940*, ed. Gershom Scholem, trans. Gary Smith and Andre Lefevere (New York: Schocken, 1989), 220–6, here 225.

17 Samuel Weber, *Benjamin's –abilities* (Cambridge, MA: Harvard University Press, 2008).

18 The historical information in this paragraph follows P. Wrzecionko, 'Erbsünde'. *Historisches Wörterbuch der Philosophie*, vol. 2, ed. Joachim Ritter (Basel: Schwabe, 1972), 604–7.

19 Most recently, in an engagement with Rembrandt's 1638 etching 'The Fall of Man', which depicts the scene of the *Erbsünde* in the Garden of Eden, Jean-Luc Nancy and Federico Ferrari open up the thinking of original sin to a certain rupture or denuding of essence: 'But sin is nudity: it is not to be clothed in the attributes of a destination, of a congruence with the order of nature and to find oneself, by contrast, given over to the task of creating an origin, of inventing one …, or even of venturing beyond all origin, that is, into the very crucible of origin: into the nudity where the origin unveils itself as what it is, that is, not as a given, not ready, not available, under way, open like the

woman's cleft at the center of the scene. Original sin: the failure to be clothed in an essence.' 'Humus', *Being Nude: The Skin of Images*, trans. Anne O'Byrne and Carlie Anglemire (New York: Fordham University Press, 2014), 41–4, here 42.

If Benjamin, through Kafka, inherits the tradition of reflecting on *Erbsünde*, it would be necessary also to consider, in a context that exceeds that of our present argumentation, the ways in which, explicitly or implicitly, the question of *Schuld* is inextricably interwoven with its history, not only in theological anthropology but also in moral philosophy. In the meantime, for a sustained reflection on the category of guilt and debt as they relate to the philosophy of history in Benjamin's thought, see Werner Hamacher, 'Schuldgeschichte. Benjamins Skizze "Kapitalismus als Religion"', in *Kapitalismus als Religion*, ed. Dirk Baecker (Berlin: Kulturverlag Kadmos, 2003), 77–119. And, from the perspective of Kafka studies, it would be fruitful to consider the problem of *Erbsünde* also in the context of Kafka's complicated relation to the Gnostic tradition. The latter relation is explored in a variety of suggestive ways by Stanley Corngold, *Lambent Traces: Franz Kafka* (Princeton: Princeton University Press, 2004).

20 Jacques Derrida, 'Before the Law', trans. Avital Ronell and Christine Roulston, in *Acts of Literature*, ed. Derek Attridge (New York: Routledge, 1992), 181–220. For a reading that links Kafka's doorkeeper episode to Benjamin's rhetoric of the 'wolkige Stelle' or 'cloudy spot', see Werner Hamacher, 'Die Geste in Namen. Benjamin und Kafka', in *Entferntes Verstehen. Studien zu Philosophie und Literatur von Kant bis Celan* (Frankfurt am Main: Suhrkamp, 1998), 280–323.

21 Benjamin, *Gesammelte Briefe*, vol. 4, 1931–4, 478–80, here 479; *Correspondence of Walter Benjamin and Gershom Scholem*, 134–6, here 135f. In a different context, Weber comments on Benjamin's statement by rightly pointing out how it 'is worth noting that Benjamin's notion of "interpretation" here involves not reproducing the essence or measure of the work as is, but rather setting it into motion.' As such, 'Benjamin's reading of Kafka does not seek to elucidate the religious doctrine that might be implicit in the work, but rather to bring out

those aspects that call for change and transformation, for a certain "movement"'. 'Violence and Gesture: Agamben Reading Benjamin Reading Kafka Reading Cervantes …' *Benjamin's –abilities*, 195–210, here 199.

22 Rodolphe Gasché, 'Kafka's Law: In the Field of Forces Between Judaism and Hellenism', *MLN* 117 (2002): 971–1002, here 980.

23 Ibid., 981.

24 The etymological remarks in this paragraph and the next are based on my discussion in *Verwaiste Hinterlassenschat. Formen gespentischen Erbens*. They draw on the entries on 'Erbe' in *Duden Etymologie. Herkunftswörterbuch der deutschen Sprache* (Mannheim: Duden, 1963), 141 and in *Etymologisches Wörterbuch des Deutschen* (Munich: DTV, 1998), 292.

25 Walter Benjamin, 'Kavaliersmoral', *Gesammelte Schriften*, vol. 4, 466–8.

26 Jacques Derrida and Elisabeth Roudinesco, *For What Tomorrow … A Dialogue*, trans. Jeff Fort (Stanford: Stanford University Press, 2004), 3.

27 Ibid.

28 Ibid., 4–5.

29 Ibid., 5–6.

30 Walter Benjamin, *Ursprung des deutschen Trauerspiels*, *Gesammelte Schriften*, vol. 1.1, 350); *The Origin of German Tragic Drama*, trans. John Osborne (London: Verso, 1998), 175.

Chapter Three

1 Johann Wolfgang Goethe, *Faust. Werke: Hamburger Ausgabe*, vol. 3, ed. Erich Trunz (Munich: Deutscher Taschenbuch Verlag, 1988), 109.

2 Nietzsche's reference is to the famous Christian theological boarding school in which Schelling, Hegel and Hölderlin were roommates. Friedrich Nietzsche, *Der Antichrist: Fluch auf das Christentum. Kritische Studienausgabe*, vol. 6, eds. Giorgio Colli and Mazzino Montinari. (Berlin: De Gruyter & Munich: Deutscher Taschenbuch Verlag, 1999), 165–254, here 176.

3 For representative overviews of the current state of scholarship

regarding the theo-political investments of Benjamin's thinking, see, among others, Eric Jacobson, *Metaphysics of the Profane: The Political Theology of Walter Benjamin and Gershom Scholem* (New York: Columbia University Press, 2003); the essay collection edited by Daniel Weidner, *Profanes Leben: Walter Benjamins Dialektik der Säkularisierung* (Frankfurt am Main: Suhrkamp, 2010); and, more recently, Michael W. Jennings, 'Towards Eschatology: The Development of Walter Benjamin's Theological Politics in the Early 1920s', in *Walter Benjamins anthropologisches Denken*, eds. Carolin Duttlinger, Ben Morgan, and Anthony Phelan (Freiburg: Rombach, 2012), 41–57. An earlier account specifically of Benjamin's relation to the Hebrew Bible is provided by Brian Britt, *Walter Benjamin and the Bible* (New York: Continuum, 1996).

4 Walter Benjamin, *Gesammelte Briefe*, vol. 4, 1931–4, 19f.; *Correspondence 1910–1940*, 371–3, here 372–3.

5 For a reading of the terms 'messianism' and 'theology' in the context of Benjamin's more overtly political thought, see Jeanne Marie Gagnebin, 'Théologie et messianisme dans la pensée de Walter Benjamin', in *Millenarismi nella cultura contemporanea—con un' appendice su yovel ebraico e giubileo cristiano*, ed. Enrico Rambaldi (Milan: Angeli, 2000), 103–15 as well as the earlier essay by Anson Rabinbach, 'Betweeen Enlightenment and Apocalypse: Benjamin, Bloch and Modern German Jewish Messianism', *New German Critique* 34 (Winter 1985): 78–124.

6 Brecht's note from his *Arbeitsjournal* is quoted in the 'documents' section of Bernd Witte's biographical and critical introduction to Benjamin, *Walter Benjamin: Mit Selbstzeugnissen und Bilddokumenten* (Reinbek bei Hamburg: Rowohlt, 1990), 145.

7 Andreas Pangritz, 'Theologie', in *Benjamins Begriffe*, eds. Michael Opitz and Erdmut Wizisla (Frankfurt am Main: Suhrkamp, 2000), 774–825.

8 Giorgio Agamben, *The Time That Remains: A Commentary on the Letter to the Romans*, trans. Patricia Dailey (Stanford: Stanford University Press, 2005), especially 138–45.

9 See Henning Günther, 'Die Bedeutung der Theologie für die Philosophie Walter Benjamins', *Neue Zeitschrift für systematische Theologie und Religionsphilosophie* 14 (1972): 141–71; Stéphane Mosès,

The Angel of History: Rosenzweig, Benjamin, Scholem, trans. Barbara Harshav. (Stanford: Stanford University Press, 2009); Josef Wohlmuth, 'Zur Bedeutung der "Geschichtsthesen" Walter Benjamins für die christliche Eschatologie', *Evangelische Theologie* 50 (1990): 2–20; and Irving Wohlfarth, 'On Some Jewish Motifs in Benjamin', in *The Problems of Modernity: Adorno and Benjamin*, ed. Andrew Benjamin (London: Routledge, 1991), 157–215.

10 Pangritz, 'Theologie', 807.

11 This is the basic thesis pursued at length in Gerhard Richter, *Walter Benjamin and the Corpus of Autobiography* (Detroit: Wayne State University Press, 2000).

12 Thomas Rentsch, 'Dialektik der Transzendenz bei Benjamin. Eine Alternative zur Substitution des Absoluten in Reflexion und Praxis der Moderne', in *Theologie und Politik: Walter Benjamin und ein Paradigma der Moderne*, ed. Bernd Witte and Mauro Ponzi with Claas Morgenroth and Karl Solibakke (Berlin: Schmidt: 2005), 32–43, here 41.

13 Benjamin, *Passagen-Werk*, 575; *Arcades Project*, 461.

14 The field of religious studies has in recent years experienced a transdisciplinary renaissance and critical expansion. Among the useful overviews of some of the basic concerns of these developments, see, for instance, John Caputo, *On Religion* (London: Routledge, 2001) and the 1,000-page volume edited by Hent de Vries, *Religion: Beyond a Concept* (New York: Fordham University Press, 2008).

15 Benjamin, *Das Passagen-Werk*, 588.

16 Benjamin, *The Arcades Project*, 471.

17 Leigh Hafrey and Richard Sieburth, trans. 'N [Re the Theory of Knowledge, Theory of Progress]', by Walter Benjamin in *Benjamin: Philosophy, Aesthetics, History*, ed. Gary Smith (Chicago: University of Chicago Press, 1989), 43–83, here 61.

18 This impasse may be understood as an instantiation of Benjamin's conviction, offered in 'The Task of the Translator', that 'to a certain degree all great texts, and, to the highest degree, the sacred ones [*die heiligen*], contain, between the lines, their virtual translation [*virtuelle Übersetzung*].' 'Die Aufgabe des Übersetzers', *Gesammelte Schriften*, vol.

4, 9–21, here 21; 'The Task of the Translator', *Selected Writings*, vol. 1, 253–63, here 263.

But the question of the virtuality of translation is, for Benjamin, far from straightforward. See Kevin McLaughlin's lucid commentary on this Benjaminan virtuality: 'For the translator, the *Gehalt* of an original is not like a substance; it is not a purified intellectual essence to be extracted.' Therefore, the 'translator does not, as Hegel and Lukács claim the philosopher does, subject the work to a process of cupellation.' Rather, for Benjamin, to encounter translation is 'a "provisional" way of coming to terms with the strangeness of language that manifests itself in translation.' 'Virtual Paris: Benjamin's Arcades Project', in *Benjamin's Ghosts: Interventions in Contemporary Literary and Cultural Theory*, ed. Gerhard Richter (Stanford: Stanford University Press, 2002), 204–25, here 208. Any translation and any consideration of an act of translation will have to situate itself in the framework of this ineluctable strangeness.

19 'Blotting Paper'. *Oxford Dictionary and Thesaurus* (New York: Oxford University Press, 1996), 147.

20 'Blotter'. *Webster's Dictionary* (Springfield, MA: Merriam-Webster, 1984), 161.

21 Here, I follow the etymological explanations provided by the Grimms' *Deutsches Wörterbuch*, vol. 12 (Leipzig: Hirzel, 1885); the *Etymologisches Wörterbuch des Deutschen*, eds. Wolfgang Pfeifer et al. (Munich: Deutscher Taschenbuch Verlag, 1997); and the *Duden Etymologie: Herkunftswörterbuch der deutschen Sprache* (Mannheim: Dudenverlag, 1963).

22 Grimm, *Deutsches Wörterbuch*, vol. 12, 1180.

23 Theodor W. Adorno and Walter Benjamin, *Briefwechsel 1928–1940*, ed. Henri Lonitz (Frankfurt am Main: Suhrkamp, 1994), 324; *The Complete Correspondence, 1928–1940*, trans. Nicolas Walker (Cambridge, MA: Harvard University Press, 1999), 249. Adorno, however, here does offer the general comment that, from his perspective, it is Benjamin's 'intention of mobilizing the power of theological experience anonymously within the profane' and that this gesture exceeds Scholem's understanding of *Rettung*, or redemptive

rescuing (ibid.). For a sustained reading of the question of *Rettung*,
cf. Gerhard Richter, 'Can Anything Be Rescued by Defending It?
Benjamin with Adorno', *differences* 31 (3) (2010): 34–52.

24 For an extended reading of the concept of mirror writing and its
relation to questions of redemption and non-redemption, cf. Gerhard
Richter, 'Aesthetic Theory and Nonpropositional Truth Content in
Adorno', *New German Critique* 97 (Winter 2006): 119–35.

25 Rodolphe Gasché, *Of Minimal Things: Studies on the Notion of Relation*
(Stanford: Stanford University Press, 1999), 5.

26 Ibid., 6f.

27 Ibid., 10.

28 Ibid., 11.

29 Nietzsche, *Der Antichrist*, 175.

30 Martin Heidegger, 'Der Spruch des Anaximander', *Holzwege*
(Frankfurt am Main: Klostermann, 1980), 317–68, here 343.

31 Jacques Derrida, 'Faith and Knowledge: The Two Sources of "Religion"
at the Limits of Reason Alone', trans. Samuel Weber, in *Religion*, eds.
Jacques Derrida and Gianni Vattimo (Stanford: Stanford University
Press, 1998), 1–78, here 60.

32 Ernst Bloch, *Atheismus im Christentum: Zur Religion des Exodus und
des Reichs*, *Werkausgabe*, vol. 14 (Frankfurt am Main: Suhrkamp,
1985), 15.

33 A different question of relation with regard to the *Löschblatt* is also
posed in Benjamin's early essay 'Eidos und Begriff' (1916), on Paul
F. Linke's phenomenological study 'Das Recht der Phänomenologie'.
There, Benjamin's sustained example for distinguishing between
concept and essence and how these two relate to each other is,
precisely, the *Löschblatt*. Benjamin, *Gesammelte Schriften*, vol. 6,
29–31.

34 The theologico-political conversation between Habermas and
Ratzinger has been published as *Dialektik der Säkularisierung: Über
Vernunft und Religion* (Freiburg: Herder, 2005).

35 Gershom Scholem, 'Offenbarung und Tradition als religiöse
Kategorien im Judentum', *Judaica: Studien zur jüdischen Mystik*, vol. 4
(Frankfurt am Main: Suhrkamp, 1984), 213.

36 Franz Kafka, *Das Schloß. Schriften und Tagebücher: Kritische Ausgabe*,
    eds. Jürgen Born, Gerhard Neumann, Malcolm Pasley and Jost
    Schillemeit (Frankfurt am Main: Fischer, 2002), 114. Scholem's and
    Kafka's passages are quoted in Bernd Witte's erudite study *Jüdische
    Tradition und literarische Moderne: Heine, Buber, Kafka, Benjamin*
    (Munich: Hanser, 2007), 219.
37 Bertolt Brecht, 'Die Frage, ob es einen Gott gibt', *Geschichten vom
    Herrn Keuner.* (Frankfurt am Main: Suhrkamp, 1971), 20.
38 Benjamin, *Passagen-Werk*, 588f.; *Arcades Project*, 471.
39 It is through the concepts of memory and remembrance, too, that one
    might trace some of the similarities between the double movement
    of preservation and erasure encrypted in Benjamin's *Löschblatt* and
    the figure of the mystic writing pad in Freud. Freud's mystic writing
    pad, or *Wunderblock*, also works to record and cancel the inscriptions
    of writing, serving as an image of the ways in which the psyche fixes
    and erases memory traces. See Freud's 1924/25 essay 'Notiz über den
    Wunderblock', *Studienausgabe*, vol. 3, eds. Alexander Mitscherlich,
    Angela Richards and James Strachey (Frankfurt am Main: Fischer,
    2000), 363–9.

Chapter Four

1 Immanuel Kant, *Kritik der reinen Vernunft, Werkausgabe*, ed. Wilhelm
   Weischedel (Frankfurt am Main: Suhrkamp, 1974), vol 3, 13; *Critique
   of Pure Reason*, trans. Paul Guyer and Allen W. Wood (Cambridge:
   Cambridge University Press, 1999), 100.
2 One of the more notable exceptions is, perhaps, the work of Italian
   philosopher Giorgio Agamben, whose texts often draw on both the
   Benjaminian and the Heideggerian traditions.
3 Berel Lang, *Heidegger's Silence* (Ithaca: Cornell University Press,
   1996), 22.
4 Walter Benjamin, *Gesammelte Briefe*, ed. Christoph Gödde and Henri
   Lonitzm vol. 3 (Frankfurt am Main: Suhrkamp, 1997), 503; *The
   Correspondence of Walter Benjamin and Gershom Scholem*, trans. Gary

Smith and André Lefevere (Cambridge, MA: Harvard University Press, 1992), 359f.

5 See Heidegger's letter to Arendt dated 10 August 1967, in which he refers to their previous meeting in July, during which they must have discussed Arendt's lecture on Benjamin. After all, Heidegger writes that on 'the day after our meeting, on Friday, July 28th, I found the passage that goes with the Mallarmé quotation in Benjamin'. In the same letter, Heidegger also registers his concern over the possibility that Arendt may have created trouble for herself by having prefaced her Freiburg lecture on Benjamin with an explicit greeting of Heidegger. Hannah Arendt and Martin Heidegger, *Briefe 1925–1975*, 3rd, exp. edn (Frankfurt am Main: Klostermann, 2002), 155f. See also the remarks by the volume's editor, Ursula Ludz, with respect to the timing of Heidegger's attendance at Arendt's Benjamin lecture following his visit with Celan and regarding the fact that Heidegger, on the day after her lecture, presented her with an inscribed copy of the Reclam version of his *The Origin of the Work of Art*. Annotations to *Briefe 1925–1975*, 322.

6 Hannah Arendt, 'Walter Benjamin: 1892–1940', Introduction to Walter Benjamin, *Illuminations: Essays and Reflections*, trans. Harry Zohn (New York: Schocken, 1985), 1–51, here 46.

7 Burkhardt Lindner, Entry on 'Das Kunstwerk im Zeitalter seiner technischen Reproduzierbarkeit', in *Benjamin-Handbuch: Leben—Werk—Wirkung*, ed. Burkhardt Lindner (Stuttgart: Metzler, 2006), 229–51, here 240.

8 For a concise differentiation of Benjamin's and Heidegger's shared non-instrumentalist view of language when compared with the premises of Carnap, Quine and others in the Anglo-Saxon analytic tradition, see Martin Seel, 'Sprache bei Benjamin und Heidegger', *Merkur* 46 (4) (April 1992): 333–40.

9 Howard Caygill, 'Benjamin, Heidegger, and the Destruction of Tradition', in *Walter Benjamin's Philosophy*, ed. Andrew Benjamin and Peter Osborne (London: Routledge, 1994), 1–31, here 1.

10 Benjamin, 'Das Leben der Studenten', *Gesammelte Schriften*, vol. 2, 75; 'The Life of the Students', *Selected Writings*, vol. 1, 38.

11 Walter Benjamin, 'Die Aufgabe des Kritikers', *Gesammelte Schriften*, vol. 6, 171–2; 'The Task of the Critic'. *Selected Writings*, vol. 2, 548–9. For a philological contextualization of this fragment in the early Benjamin's work, see Uwe Steiner, *Die Geburt der Kritik aus dem Geiste der Kunst: Untersuchungen zum Begriff der Kritik in den frühen Schriften Walter Benjamins* (Würzburg: Königshausen & Neumann, 1989), 263.

12 Benjamin, *Gesammelte Briefe*, vol. 1, 389; *Correspondence*, 97.

13 Benjamin, *Gesammelte Briefe*, vol. 2, 208; *Correspondence*, 194.

14 Uwe Steiner makes this observation in 'Kritik', in *Benjamins Begriffe*, ed. Michael Opitz and Erdmut Wizisla (Frankfurt am Main: Suhrkamp, 2000), 479–523, here 498.

15 Benjamin, 'Goethes Wahlverwandtschaften', *Gesammelte Schriften*, vol. 1, 125; 'Goethe's Elective Affinities', *Selected Writings*, vol. 1, 297.

16 'Goethes Wahlverwandtschaften', 126; 'Goethe's Elective Affinities', 298.

17 For a sustained discussion of Fichte's and Herder's transformations of the Kantian system of critique, see Kurt Röttgers, *Kritik und Praxis: Zur Geschichte des Kritikbegriffs von Kant bis Marx* (Berlin: de Gruyter, 1975).

18 Friedrich Schlegel, 'Vom Wesen der Kritik', in *Schriften zur Literatur*, ed. Wolfdietrich Rasch (Munich: Deutscher Taschenbuch Verlag, 1985), 250–9, here 259; 'Concerning the Essence of Critique', trans. Andreas Michel and Assenka Oksiloff, in *Theory as Practice: A Critical Anthology of Early German Romantic Writings*, eds. Jochen Schulte-Sasse et al. (Minneapolis: University of Minnesota Press, 1997), 268–77, here 276f.

19 Bernd Witte, *Walter Benjamin: Der Intellektuelle als Kritiker— Untersuchungen zu seinem Frühwerk* (Stuttgart: Metzler, 1976), 5.

20 Benjamin, *Gesammelte Schriften*, vol. 1, 52; *Selected Writings*, vol. 1, 142.

21 Benjamin, *Pasagen-Werk*, 274; *Arcades Project*, 207.

22 Rolf Tiedemann, 'Dialectics at a Standstill: Approaches to the Passagen-Werk', trans. Gary Smith and André Lefevere, in *On Walter Benjamin: Critical Essays and Reflections*, ed. Gary Smith (Cambridge, MA: MIT Press, 1988), 260–91, here 281.

23   Benjamin, *Passagen-Werk*, 580; *Arcades Project*, 464.

24   Benjamin, 'Goethes Wahlverwandtschaften', 156; 'Goethe's Elective Affinities', 298.

25   Dorothea Kimmich, *Lebendige Dinge in der Moderne* (Konstanz: Konstanz University Press, 2011), 55. Kimmich's study as a whole provides a sensitive reading of literary modernity and the thing.

26   Ibid. For a reading of Benjamin's image of the sock in relation to his preferred literary and philosophical genre of the *Denkbild*, see the discussion of 'The Sock' from the *Berlin Childhood around 1900* in Gerhard Richter, *Thought-Images: Frankfurt School Writers' Reflections from Damaged Life* (Stanford: Stanford University Press, 2007), 9–11.

27   Kimmich, 58.

28   Benjamin, *Einbahnstraße, Gesammelte Schriften*, vol. 4, 93; *Selected Writings*, vol. 1, 449. For a reading of 'Construction Site' in the context of Benjamin's political montage, see Michael W. Jennings, 'Trugbild der Stabilität. Weimarer Politik und Montage-Theorie in Benjamins *Einbahnstraße*', trans. Gerhard Richter and Michael W. Jennings, *Gobal Benjamin*, vol. 1, ed. Klaus Garber and Ludger Rehm (Munich: Fink, 1999), 517–28.

29   I analyse this imbrication in detail in 'Benjamin's Ear: Noise, Mnemonics, and the Berlin Chronicle', *Walter Benjamin and the Corpus of Autobiography* (Detroit: Wayne State University Press, 2000), 163–97.

30   Benjamin, *Passagen-Werk*, 272; *Arcades Project*, 205.

31   Benjamin, *Passagen-Werk*, 273; *Arcades Project*, 206.

32   Benjamin, *Gesammelte Schriften*, vol. 3, 198; *Selected Writings*, vol. 2, 265.

33   A sustained reading of the gaze in relation to its objects can be found in Gerhard Richter, 'Benjamin's Eye/I: Vision and the Scene of Writing in the Berlin Chronicle around 1900', *Walter Benjamin and the Corpus of Autobiography*, 199–229.

34   Benjamin, *Gesammelte Schriften*, vol. 1, 110; *Selected Writings*, vol. 1, 178f.

35   Samuel Weber, *Benjamin's -abilities* (Cambridge, MA: Harvard University Press, 2008).

36 G. W. F. Hegel, *Phenomenology of Spirit*, trans. A. V. Miller (Oxford: Oxford University Press, 1979), 66; *Phänomenologie des Geistes*, Werke, vol. 3 (Frankfurt am Main: Suhrkamp, 1986), 91f.

37 Hegel, *Phenomenology*, 74; *Phänomenologie*, 101f.

38 Benjamin, *Gesammelte Schriften*, vol. 1, 350; *The Origin of the German Tragic Drama*, trans. John Osborne (London: Verso, 1998), 175.

39 Benjamin, *Gesammelte Schriften*, vol. 1, 333f.; *The Origin of the German Tragic Drama*, 156f.

40 For a fuller reading of Dürer's woodcut in the context of Benjamin's and the artist Anselm Kiefer's angelology, see Gerhard Richter, 'History's Flight, Anselm Kiefer's Angels'. *Connecticut Review* 24 (1) (Spring 2002): 113–36.

41 A general discussion of 'the expressionless' in Benjamin is offered by Winfried Menninghaus, 'Das Ausdruckslose: Walter Benjamins Kritik des Schönen durch das Erhabene', in *Walter Benjamin 1892–1940*, ed. Uwe Steiner (Bern: Lang, 1992), 33–76.

42 See, for instance, the comprehensive and learned volumes *Heidegger-Handbuch: Leben—Werk—Wirkung*, ed. Dieter Thomä (Stuttgart: Metzler, 2003); *The Cambridge Companion to Heidegger*, 2nd edn, ed. Charles Guignon (Cambridge: Cambridge University Press, 2006); and *A Companion to Heidegger*, eds. Hubert Dreyfus and Mark Wrathall (Oxford: Blackwell, 2005).

43 See the essays and statements collected in Herbert Marcuse, *Heideggerean Marxism* (Lincoln: University of Nebraska Press, 2005).

44 Martin Heidegger, 'Brief über den "Humanismus"'. *Gesamtausgabe* (Frankfurt am Main: Vittorio Klosterman, 1974), vol. 9, 339f.; 'Letter on Humanism', trans. Frank Capuzzi, in *Pathmarks*, ed. William McNeill (Cambridge: Cambridge University Press, 1998), 239–76, here 258f.

45 Fred Dallmayr, *Between Freiburg and Frankfurt: Toward a Critical Ontology* (Amherst: University of Massachusetts Press, 1991), 27.

46 Ibid., 31.

47 Heidegger, 'Das Ende der Philosophie und die Aufgabe des Denkens', *Gesamtausgabe*, vol. 14, 69; 'The End of Philosophy and the Task of Thinking', trans. Joan Stambaugh, *Basic Writings*, rev. and exp. edn

David Farrell Krell (San Francisco: HarperCollins, 1993), 427–49, here 431.

48 Heidegger, 'Das Ende der Philosophie', 82; 'The End of Philosophy', 444.

49 Heidegger, 'Das Ende der Philosophie', 86; 'The End of Philosophy', 446.

50 Heidegger, 'Das Ende der Philosophie', 90; 'The End of Philosophy', 449.

51 Kant, *Kritik der reinen Vernunft*, 29f.; *Critique of Pure Reason*, 114f.

52 I borrow the remaining lines of this paragraph along with the following two paragraphs from my *Afterness: Figures of Following in Modern Thought and Aesthetics* (New York: Columbia University Press, 2011), where they appear in a slightly different version.

53 Rodolphe Gasché, *The Honor of Thinking: Critique, Theory, Philosophy* (Stanford: Stanford University Press, 2007), 13. See also Klaus Düsing, 'Immanuel Kant. Aufklärung und Kritik', in *Philosophen des 18. Jahrhunderts. Eine Einführung*, ed. Lothar Kreimendahl (Darmstadt: WBG, 2000).

54 My understanding here is indebted to Gasché's insightful interpretation of this Heideggerian passage in *The Honor of Thinking*, 14.

55 Heidegger, *Gesamtausgabe*, vol. 41, 121f.; *What Is a Thing?*, trans. W. B. Barton, Jr. and Vera Deutsch (Chicago: Regnery, 1968), 119f.

56 Benjamin, *Gesammelte Schriften*, vol. 1, 78; *Selected Writings*, vol. 1, 159.

57 Heidegger, *Gesamtausgabe*, vol. 41, 122; *What Is a Thing?*, 120.

58 Heidegger, *Gesamtausgabe*, vol. 41, 122; *What Is a Thing?*, 120.

59 Heidegger, *Gesamtausgabe*, vol. 41, 123; *What Is a Thing?*, 122.

60 Heidegger, *Gesamtausgabe*, vol. 41, 125; *What Is a Thing?*, 123.

61 Kant, *Critique of Pure Reason*, 115; *Kritik der Urteilskraft*, 31.

62 Walter Biemel, 'Die Entfaltung von Heideggers Ding-Begriff', *Gesammelte Schriften* (Stuttgart – Bad Cannstatt: Frommann-Holzboog, 1996), vol. 1, 353–78, here 356.

63 Heidegger, *Gesamtausgabe*, vol. 41, 55; *What Is a Thing?*, 55.

64 Heidegger, *Gesamtausgabe*, vol. 41, 56; *What Is a Thing?*, 56.

65 Heidegger, *Gesamtausgabe*, vol. 41, 61f.; *What Is a Thing?*, 61f.

66 Heidegger, *Gesamtausgabe*, vol. 41, 119f.; *What Is a Thing?*, 118f.

67 Martin Heidegger, *Gesamtausgabe*, vol. 5, 3; 'The Origin of the Work of Art', trans. Albert Hofstadter, *Basic Writings*, 143–212, here 144.

68 Martin Heidegger, *Gesamtausgabe*, vol. 5, 3; 'The Origin of the Work of Art', 145.

69 See the reflections collected in Jacques Lacan, *The Seminar of Jacques Lacan, Book VII: The Ethics of Psychoanalysis 1959–1960*, ed. Jacques-Alain Miller, trans. Dennis Porter (New York: Norton, 1992), especially the section entitled 'Introduction to the Thing' (17–84). It will be necessary, in another context, to trace the similarities and differences between Heidegger and Lacan as they converge on *das Ding*. In his seminar, Lacan leaves much interpretative work for his readers to accomplish when he contents himself with a passing reference to Heidegger's *Ding* in general: 'To have confirmation of the appropriation of the vase for this purpose, look up what Heidegger affirms when he writes about *das Ding*. He's the last in a long line to have meditated on the subject of creation; and he develops his dialectic around a vase. I will not be concerned here with the function of *das Ding* in Heidegger's approach to the contemporary revelation of what he calls Being and that is linked to the end of metaphysics … You will see the function Heidegger assigns it [*das Ding*] of uniting celestial and terrestrial powers around it in an essential human process' (120).

70 Heidegger, *Gesamtausgabe*, vol. 5, 20; 'The Origin of the Work of Art', 160.

71 Heidegger, *Gesamtausgabe*, vol. 5, 25; 'The Origin of the Work of Art', 165. In another discussion, it would be illuminating to consider Heidegger's emphasis on the movement of the work leading to the thing – rather than vice versa – also in relation to the framework of his more general understanding of physicality. A suggestive start has been made by the philosopher Charles E. Scott, *The Lives of Things* (Bloomington: Indiana University Press, 2002), 57–67, who locates Heidegger's general idea of physicality in the context of his post-Husserlian understanding of the phenomenological concept of *Lebenswelt*.

72 Martin Heidegger, *Gesamtausgabe* 79, 7f.; 'The Thing', trans. Albert Hofstadter, *Poetry, Language, Thought*, ed. Albert Hofstadter (New York: Perennial Classics, 2001), 161–84, here 166f.
73 Martin Heidegger, *Gesamtausgabe* 79, 14; 'The Thing', 173.
74 Martin Heidegger, *Gesamtausgabe* 79, 20; 'The Thing', 179.
75 By contrast, a Heideggerean thinking of thingliness always also involves a rigorous reconsideration of what it is that causes us to speak of someone as human or of something as an object endowed with this or that meaning. The thing cannot but be inscribed in the attitudes through which we relate to objects, and by extension, to being-in-the-world itself. As Hubert Dreyfus eloquently observes in his engagement with Heidegger: 'Our everyday know-how involves an understanding of what it is to be a person, a thing, a natural object, a plant, an animal, and so on. Our understanding of animals these days, for example, is in part embodied in our skill in buying pieces of them, taking off their plastic wrapping, and cooking them in microwave ovens. In general, we deal with things as resources to be used and then disposed of when no longer needed. A Styrofoam cup is a perfect example. When we want a hot or cold drink it does its job, and when we are through with it we throw it away. This understanding of an object is very different from what we can suppose to be the Japanese understanding of a delicate, painted teacup, which does not do as good a job of maintaining temperature and which has to be washed and protected, but which is preserved from generation to generation for its beauty and social meaning. Or, to take another example, an old earthenware bowl, admired for its simplicity and its ability to evoke memories of ancient crafts, such as is used in a Japanese tea ceremony, embodies a unique understanding of things. It is hard to picture a tea ceremony around a Styrofoam cup.' 'Heidegger on the Connection between Nihilism, Art, Technology, and Politics', *The Cambridge Companion to Heidegger*, 2nd edn, ed. Charles Guignon (Cambridge: Cambridge University Press, 2006), 345–72, here 351. One might add that this also would be one of the conceptual conjunctions between late Heidegger's reading of the thing and his critique of the *Ge-stell*, the technical enframement through which objects, and the world as

such, become mere entities of an omnipresent *Be-stand*, a standing
reserve or stockpile, in which everything, having lost the capacity for
distance, absence, and singularity, can simply be placed on order –
becomes, that is, with every placed order a treacherous affirmation of
the modern world's principle orderability.

76   Rainer Maria Rilke, *Briefe* (Frankfurt am Main: Insel, 1987), vol. 1, 61.
77   See John Sallis, *Stone* (Bloomington: Indiana University Press,
     1994) and Alphonso Lingis, *The Imperative* (Bloomington: Indiana
     University Press, 1998), especially the remarkable sections on the
     intimate and alien nature of things and on their production, pageantry
     and purpose (73–102).
78   Max Horkheimer, 'Traditional and Critical Theory', trans. Matthew
     J. O'Connell, *Critical Theory: Selected Essays* (New York: Continuum,
     1999), 188–243.
79   Theodor W. Adorno, 'Kritik', *Gesammelte Schriften*, ed. Rolf
     Tiedemann (Frankfurt am Main: Suhrkamp, 1997), vol. 10, 785–93,
     here 791; 'Critique', *Critical Models: Interventions and Catchwords*, ed.
     and trans. Henry Pickford (New York: Columbia University Press,
     1998), 281–8, here 286.
80   Michel Foucault, 'What Is Critique?', *The Essential Foucault*, eds. Paul
     Rabinow and Nikolas Rose (New York: New Press, 2003), 263–78.
81   Ibid, 265.
82   Jacques Derrida, 'A "Madness" Must Watch Over Thinking', trans.
     Peggy Kamuf, *Points … Interviews, 1974–1994*, ed. Elizabeth Weber
     (Stanford: Stanford University Press, 1995), 338–64, here 357. In
     an investigation that exceeds the boundaries of the current project,
     it also will be fruitful to engage at length with the few pages that
     Derrida devotes to Heidegger's thinking of the thing in relation to the
     constellation of the animal, mortality, death and sovereignty, the topics
     of Derrida's last seminars. See specifically the opening 'detour' of
     Derrida's seminar on 5 February 2003, in *The Beast and the Sovereign*,
     vol. 2, eds. Michel Lisse, Marie-Louise Mallet and Ginette Michaud,
     trans. Geoffrey Bennington (Chicago: University of Chicago Press,
     2011), 119–26. For an incisive analysis of Derrida's consideration of
     animality in these seminars, cf. David Farrell Krell, *Derrida and Our*

Animal Others: Derrida's Final Seminar, 'The Beast and the Sovereign'
(Bloomington: Indiana University Press, 2013).

83 This is the argument made throughout Willem van Reijen, *Der
Schwarzwald und Paris: Heidegger und Benjamin* (Munich: Fink,
1998). It is plausible, however, to redraw the political divisions
between Benjamin and Heidegger along the interpretative lines of
specific conceptions of philosophical issues in their work, such as
their divergent views of time and historicity. For an extended analysis
of Benjamin's and Heidegger's perspectives on the conjunction of
art and historicity, see Stefan Knoche, *Benjamin—Heidegger: Über
Gewalt – Die Politisierung der Kunst* (Vienna: Turia & Kant, 2000).
Cf. Andrew Benjamin's suggestive observation that their differing
concepts of what constitutes the present allow us to appreciate the
extent to which 'the ineliminable presence of a different politics …
can be reworked as the primordial conflict over the nature of the
present … . What is proposed is a conflict that cannot be resolved
by a simple deferral to the instant. The conflict between Benjamin
and Heidegger is political for precisely this reason.' 'Time and
Task: Benjamin and Heidegger Showing the Present', *Present Hope:
Philosophy, Architecture, Judaism* (London: Routledge, 1997), 26–55,
here 28.

Chapter Five

1 Walter Benjamin, *Gesammelte Briefe, Band 3: 1925–1930*, 159;
Correspondence, 300.

2 Susan Sontag, 'Under the Sign of Saturn', *Under the Sign of Saturn*
(New York: Farrar, Straus & Giroux, 1980), 109–34, here 129.

3 Walter Benjamin, *Der Begriff der Kunstkritik in der deutschen
Romantik, Gesammelte Schriften*, vol. 1, 42; 'The Concept of Criticism
in German Romanticism', *Selected Writings*, vol. 1, 116–200, here 136.

4 Walter Benjamin, *Ursprung des deutschen Trauerspiels, Gesammelte
Schriften*, vol. 1, 207; *The Origin of German Tragic Drama*, 27.

5 Samuel Weber, 'Benjamin's Writing Style', *Encyclopedia of Aesthetics*, ed. Michael Kelly (Oxford: Oxford University Press, 1998), 261–4, here 262f.

6 Walter Benjamin, 'Das Kunstwerk im Zeitalter seiner technischen Reproduzierbarkeit (Dritte Fassung)', *Gesammelte Schriften*, eds. Rolf Tiedemann and Hermann Schweppenhäuser (Frankfurt am Main: Suhrkamp, 1991), vol. 1, 471–508, here 478; 'The Work of Art in the Age of Its Technological Reproducibility (Third Version)', *Selected Writings*, vol. 4, 251–83, here 255.

7 Many of Benjamin's writings dealing with media-related questions, writings which are often embedded in texts whose apparent topic or object seems to have little to do with media-specific questions or with problems of mediality, are now thoughtfully collected and contextualized in Walter Benjamin, *Medienästhetische Schriften*, ed. Detlev Schöttker (Frankfurt am Main: Suhrkamp, 2002) and, in English, in Walter Benjamin, *The Work of Art in the Age of Its Technological Reproducibility and Other Writings on Media*, eds. Michael W. Jennings, Brigid Doherty and Thomas Y. Levin (Cambridge, MA: Harvard University Press, 2008).

8 Burkhardt Lindner, 'Medienwissenschaft', *Benjamin-Handbuch: Leben—Werk—Wirkung*, ed. Burkhardt Lindner (Stuttgart: Metzler, 2006), 46–9, here 46.

9 In a polemical essay, in which he fluctuates between the question of whether Benjamin assimilated enough Marx and the question of whether it was in some way less than advantageous for Benjamin's own method to have assimilated as much of Marx's historical materialism as he did, the art historian T. J. Clark claims that '"Marxist method" never got under his [Benjamin's] skin … But none of this means that Benjamin's Marxism, such as it was, did not feed and enliven the project he had in hand'. 'Should Benjamin Have Read Marx?', *Boundary 2* 30 (1) (2003), 31–49, here 41.

10 Friedrich Nietzsche, *Jenseits von Gut und Böse; Zur Genealogie der Moral, Kritische Studienausgabe*, eds. Giorgio Colli and Mazzino Montinari, vol. 5 (Munich: Deutscher Taschenbuch Verlag and Berlin: de Gruyter, 1999), 317.

11 Immanuel Kant, *Kritik der Urteilskraft, Werkausgabe*, ed. Wilhelm

Weischedel, vol. 10 (Frankfurt am Main: Suhrkamp, 1974), 74f.;
Critique of the Power of Judgment, trans. Paul Guyer and Eric
Matthews (Cambridge: Cambridge University Press, 2000), 56.

12   We should note that, next to the cognitive specificity of aesthetic
experience, Benjamin also engages on multiple levels with the concept
of the Kantian *idea*. As Michael W. Jennings has pointed out, Benjamin
does not always clearly differentiate between the various notions of the
idea as they occur in Plato, Kant and Fichte. For Jennings, 'Benjamin's
debt to Kant' is that 'in the face of the arbitrary, disjunctive nature
of human experience and the fixed limitations of human cognitive
capacity, it is our involvement with language—as ideas—which can
potentially integrate and give meaning to our experience.' *Dialectical
Images: Walter Benjamin's Theory of Literary Criticism* (Ithaca: Cornell
University Press, 1987), 201. For a reading of Benjamin's theory of the
idea in the context of Plato, Kant, Hegel, Jena Romanticism and Jewish
mysticism, compare further Hans Heinz Holz, 'Idee', *Benjamins Begriffe*,
eds. Michael Opitz and Erdmut Wizisla (Frankfurt am Main: Suhrkamp,
2000), vol. 2, 445–78. Finally, for an analysis of Benjamin's idea of
historical time in relation to Kant's, see Werner Hamacher, '"Jetzt":
Benjamin zur historischen Zeit', *Benjamin Studien* 1 (2002), 145–83.

13   Nietzsche, *Jenseits von Gut und Böse; Zur Genealogie der Moral,
Kritische Studienausgabe*, vol. 5, 152.

14   For a general consideration of the relation between Benjamin and
Nietzsche, see Helmut Pfotenhauer, 'Benjamin und Nietzsche', *Walter
Benjamin im Kontext*, 2nd edn, ed. Burkhardt Lindner (Königstein/Ts:
Athenäum, 1985), 100–26.

15   Gershom Scholem, *Walter Benjamin—die Geschichte einer
Freundschaft* (Frankfurt am Main: Suhrkamp, 1990), 78. Partially cited
in Pfotenhauer, 103.

16   Scholem, *Freundschaft*, 78.

17   I am thinking, among others, of Rodolphe Gasché, 'Objective
Diversions: On Some Kantian Themes in Benjamin's "The Work of
Art in the Age of Mechanical Reproduction"', in *Walter Benjamin's
Philosophy: Destruction and Experience*, eds. Andrew Benjamin and
Peter Osborne (London: Routledge, 1994); Howard Caygill, *Walter*

Benjamin: The Colour of Experience (London: Routledge, 1994); and Peter Fenves, "'Über das Programm der kommenden Philosophie'", trans. Markus Hardtmann, in *Benjamin-Handbuch: Leben—Werk—Wirkung*, ed. Burkhardt Lindner (Stuttgart: Metzler, 2006), 134–50.

18 Walter Benjamin, *Passagen-Werk*, 575; *Arcades Project*, 461.

19 *Passagen-Werk*, 593; *Arcades Project*, 474.

20 Friedrich Nietzsche, 'Über Wahrheit und Lüge im aussermoralischen Sinne', *Kritische Studienausgabe*, vol. 1, 872–90, here 882.

21 Walter Benjamin, 'Ein Außenseiter macht sich bemerkbar: Zu S. Kracauer, "Die Angestellten"', *Gesammelte Schriften*, vol. 3, 219–25, here 225; 'An Outsider Makes His Mark', *Selected Writings*, vol. 2, 305–11, here 310. Kracauer, for his part, remained invariably proud of Benjamin's designation throughout his life. See, for instance, Kracauer's letter to Adorno dated 28 August 1954, in which he writes, in relation to the topic of Kafka and garbage as it is thematized in Adorno's essay on Kafka, that 'Benjamin once said something similar about me: in his great review of *Die Angestellten* he compared me to a rag-picker who arrives at dawn to pick up the refuse.' Theodor W. Adorno and Siegfried Kracauer, *Briefwechsel 1923-1966*, ed. Wolfgang Schopf (Frankfurt am Main: Suhrkamp, 2008), 470.

22 These concerns also would have to be related to Jacques Derrida's reflections, in so many of his texts from the late 1980s and 1990s, on the politico-theological challenge of thinking a messianicity without a messiah, a messianicity without messianism. In short, for Derrida, who develops these notions partially in relation to Benjamin, the thinking of a messianicity without messianism would work to keep hope-saturated, future-directed inscriptions of a certain theological thought alive *structurally* without reducing it to the history of actual messianisms and the empirical genealogies of messiah-based political theologies. For a recent consideration of Benjamin's messianism in relation to Derrida's also see Michael G. Levine, *A Weak Messianic Power: Figures of a Time to Come in Benjamin, Derrida, and Celan* (New York: Fordham University Press, 2013).

23 Walter Benjamin, 'Franz Kafka. Zur zehnten Wiederkehr seines Todestages', *Gesammelte Schriften*, vol. 2, 409–38, here 428; 'Franz

Kafka. On the Tenth Anniversary of His Death', *Selected Writings*, vol. 2, 794–818, here, 808.

24 Benjamin, *Das Passagen-Werk*, 574; *The Arcades Project*, 460.

25 Benjamin, 'Das Kunstwerk', 473; 'The Work of Art', 252.

26 I develop this idea of the political in relation to Benjamin's confessional and autobiographical texts at length in *Walter Benjamin and the Corpus of Autobiography* (Detroit: Wayne State University Press, 2000) and in 'Acts of Self-Portraiture: Benjamin's Confessional and Literary Writings', *The Cambridge Companion to Walter Benjamin*, ed. David S. Ferris (Cambridge: Cambridge University Press, 2004), 221–37.

27 Alain Badiou, 'Fifteen Theses on Contemporary Art', *Inaesthetik* 0 (June 2008), 11–26, here 26.

28 Ibid., 24.

29 Benjamin, 'Das Kunstwerk', 473; ; 'The Work of Art', 252.

30 Benjamin, 'An Gretel Karplus und Theodor Wiesengrund Adorno, 16 August 1935', *Gesammelte Briefe, Band V: 1935–1937*, eds. Christoph Gödde und Henri Lonitz (Frankfurt am Main; Suhrkamp, 1999), 141–6, here 143; *Correspondence*, 506–8, here 506–7.

31 Benjamin, *Das Passagen-Werk*, 578; *The Arcades Project*, 463.

Chapter Six

1 Translated from the German by Stephanie S. Richter.

2 Johann Wolfgang Goethe, 'Maximen und Reflexionen', *Werke* (Hamburger Ausgabe), vol. 12, eds. Werner Weber, Hans Joachim Schrimpf and Herbert von Einem (Munich: Beck, 1988), 470; *Maxims and Reflections*, trans. Elisabeth Stopp (London: Penguin, 1999), 171. On occasion, translations of non-English sources have been slightly adjusted. (Trans.)

3 Edgar Allan Poe, 'The Facts in the Case of M. Valdemar', *The Complete Works*, vol. 5 (New York: AMS, 1965), 154–66, here 163.

4 Roland Barthes, *Camera Lucida: Reflections on Photography*, trans. Richard Howard (New York: Hill and Wang, 1993), 96.

5 Ibid.

6 Ibid., 97.

7 Walter Benjamin, 'Franz Kafka. Zur zehnten Wiederkehr seines Todestages'. *Gesammelte Schriften*, vol. 2, 409–38, here 416; 'Franz Kafka: On the Tenth Anniversary of His Death', trans. Harry Zohn, *Selected Writings*, vol. 2, 794–818, here 800. Benjamin's reflections on Kafka's photograph can be said to belong to a more general economy of a certain 'image withdrawal' that is operative in Benjamin's writings. See Gerhard Richter, 'Afterness and the Image (II): Image Withdrawal', *Afterness: Figures of Following in Modern Thought and Aesthetics* (New York: Columbia University Press, 2011), 139–53.

8 Franz Kafka, 'Josefine, die Sängerin oder das Volk der Mäuse', *Kritische Ausgabe: Drucke zu Lebzeiten*, ed. Wolf Kittler, Hans-Gerd Koch, and Gerhard Neumann (Frankfurt am Main: Fischer, 2002), 366; 'Josephine, the Singer or The Mouse People', *Selected Stories*, ed. and trans. Stanley Corngold (New York: Norton, 2007), 94–108, here 103.

9 Ludwig Wittgenstein, *Philosophische Untersuchungen*, vol. 1, eds. G. E. M. Anscombe and R. Rhees (Frankfurt am Main: Suhrkamp, 1977), 115; *Philosophical Investigations*, 4th edn, trans. Gertrude Anscombe, Peter Hacker and Joachim Schulte (West Sussex: Wiley-Blackwell, 2009), 53e.

10 Siegfried Kracauer, 'Die Photographie', *Das Ornament der Masse* (Frankfurt am Main: Suhrkamp, 1977), 21–39, here 25f.; 'Photography', *The Mass Ornament: Weimar Essays*, ed. and trans. Thomas Y. Levin (Cambridge, MA: Harvard University Press, 1995), 47–63, here 51.

11 'Die Photographie', 26; 'Photography', 51.

12 'Die Photographie', 23; 'Photography', 49.

13 'Die Photographie', 23; 'Photography', 49.

14 Elsewhere, this perspective on fashion and the problem of its readability would deserve to be expanded by taking recourse to Paul de Man's far-reaching insight: 'Fashion is like the ashes left behind by the uniquely shaped flames of the fire, the trace alone revealing that a fire actually took place.' 'Literary History and Literary Modernity', *Blindness and Insight: Essays in the Rhetoric of Contemporary Criticism*, 2nd edn (Minneapolis: University of Minnesota Press, 1983), 142–65, here 147.

Index